SCHOLASTIC

Better Than Book Reports

Christine Boardman Moen

NEW YORK • TORONTO • LONDON • AUCKLAND • SYDNEY
MEXICO CITY • NEW DELHI • HONG KONG • BUENOS AIRES

Teaching Resources

Dedication

This book is lovingly dedicated to my miraculous granddaughter, Katelyn.

Acknowledgment

A special thank you to Dr. Roxanne Owens of DePaul University as well as Nikki Crancer, Katie Deal, Jacqueline Mileusnic, and their 3rd, 4th, and 5th grade students at Alphonsus Academy and Center for the Arts in Chicago, Illinois.

Seek, Nurture, and Excite the Reader Inside Every Student!

—CBM

Editor: Sarah Longhi
Content editing by Rebecca Callan
Designed by Melinda Belter
Cover design by Jason Robinson
Cover artwork by Elizabeth Tredeau
Illustrations on page 66 from *Origami Math, Grades 2–3* by Karen Baicker (Scholastic, 2004) used with permission.

ISBN-13: 978-0-545-14320-2
ISBN-10: 0-545-14320-9

Contents

INTRODUCTION

ACTIVITY IDEAS

SMALL GROUP BOOK-SHARING ACTIVITIES

ASSESSMENT TOOLS

Introduction

Welcome to *Better Than Book Reports,* a resource used for over 15 years by teachers and students in classrooms worldwide. I feel privileged to have revised and updated this edition for you and hope that you will turn to the book-sharing activities on these pages again and again.

—Christine Boardman Moen

About This Book

Each of the book-sharing activities in this book is intended as a student "comprehension demonstration." They are designed to go beyond a tiresome, repetitive book report format and invite students to share their love of books by reading, writing, listening, speaking, and thinking critically.

To make lesson planning and navigating each activity easier, information for teachers appears on teacher pages along with book lists and an overview of a suggested approach to the Demonstration & Guided Practice session. Each session shows how to model the completion of a specific book-sharing activity and provide students with guided practice in the same way a think-aloud is used to model different reading strategies. Reproducible student pages include all necessary directions and information so students can independently complete book-sharing activities. Finally, a grading

rubric and self-assessment form are included on pages 126 and 127 to help you evaluate students' work. For a closer look at the teacher pages and reproducible student pages, refer to the featured activity below.

Connections to the Standards

Engaging students in purposeful activities that support learning standards is at the foundation of this resource. You'll find a list of key language arts standards and descriptors compiled from the work of professional organizations, such as the International Reading Association, and from state standards lists. To find activities that target a specific standard, refer to the Standards Matrix on pages 8 and 9. This matrix also helps you locate activities that support the types of texts you want students to use: fiction, nonfiction, poetry, biography, and blended books (narrative stories with facts woven in).

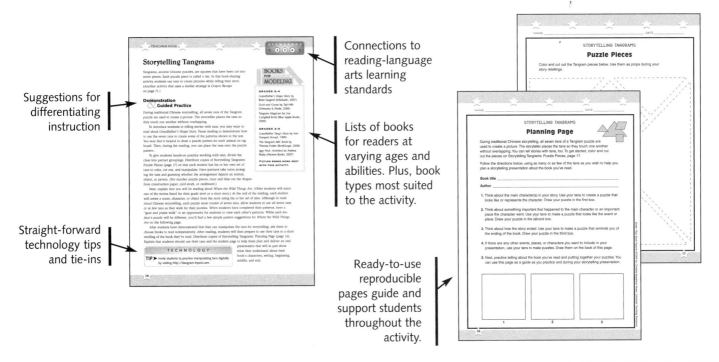

Suggestions for differentiating instruction

Straight-forward technology tips and tie-ins

Connections to reading-language arts learning standards

Lists of books for readers at varying ages and abilities. Plus, book types most suited to the activity.

Ready-to-use reproducible pages guide and support students throughout the activity.

Standards That Target Reading-Response Skills and Concepts

Students Will Be Able to . . .

STANDARD 1: WRITING

- Write in complete sentences.
- Write lists, descriptions, explanations, notes, dialogue, and brief stories.
- Supply information to complete story frames and graphic organizers.
- Summarize or paraphrase information in writing.
- Create and then answer story math problems.
- Create summary titles and write addresses.

STANDARD 2: READING

- Comprehend and follow written directions.
- Comprehend different types of text structures and genres.
- Identify and explain literary elements as well as examples of literary language.
- Comprehend and explain the use of dialogue and its purpose.
- Comprehend, locate, and supply synonyms for vocabulary words.
- Make predictions, reread for understanding, and determine point of view.

STANDARD 3: LISTENING AND SPEAKING

- Plan, practice, and deliver oral presentations for different purposes/audiences.
- Listen for important, interesting details and follow oral instructions.

STANDARD 4: UTILIZING VISUAL/MEDIA LITERACY

- Use manipulatives for various purposes such as retelling a story.
- Accurately complete instructions composed of visuals.
- Operate media devices and integrate media-created products into presentations.
- Read a map and use it to plot or trace a route.
- Utilize photographs and illustrations for descriptive purposes.

STANDARD 5: CONDUCTING RESEARCH/ EXAMINING TEXT IN DETAIL

- Search for information within the text of their chosen book.
- Search for additional information in print and non-print sources.
- Select appropriate information suitable for their book-sharing activity.

MORE INFORMATION ON STANDARDS

Helping students meet benchmarks for learning is an important part of curriculum design, lesson planning, and classroom practice. For more information about how to help the students you teach meet the standards, consider surveying what your state, other states, and national education organizations are doing to that end. One of the most comprehensive, searchable lists of standards can be found at http://www.mcrel.org, the site of Midcontinent Research for Education and Learning (McREL).

Find activities that meet the standards you're teaching (pages 8–9).

Standards Matrix

Use this matrix in your planning as you select texts and standards on which to focus.

SUGGESTED ACTIVITIES	BOOK TYPE	WRITING 1	READING 2	SPEAKING AND LISTENING 3	UTILIZING VISUAL/MEDIA LITERACY 4	CONDUCTING RESEARCH/ EXAMINING TEXT IN DETAIL 5
Culture Kits	F, NF, BL					
Storytelling Tangrams	F	X	X			
Story Trees	F		X			
A One-Person Show	F, BL		X	X		
Experience the Experiment	F, NF, BL	X	X			
Creative Catalogs	F, NF, BL	X	X	X		
Recipes for Good Books	F, NF, BL	X	X		X	
Seeing Math	F, NF, BL	X	X			
Fitting the Character to a T	F, NF	X	X			
Plot Puzzles	F, NF, BL	X			X	
All in a Day's Work	F, BL	X	X			
Two-Person Performances	NF	X	X	X		X
Story Maps	F, P	X	X		X	
The What Chart	F, BL	X	X			
Double-Duty Dictionaries	NF, BL	X	X		X	X
Problems and Solutions	F, BL	X	X		X	X
SWBS: A Plot Chart	F	X	X			X
PERSONification Webs						
Opinion Pages	F		X			
Notable Quotables	F, NF, BL	X	X		X	X
Synonym Strips	F, NF, BL	X	X			
Thank You Notes	F, NF, BL	X	X			
Cause-and-Effect Organizers	F, NF, BL	X	X			
Add-On Stories	F, NF, BL	X	X		X	
Research-Based ABC Books	F		X		X	X
Words for Wordless Books	F, NF	X	X		X	
Pattern Poetry	F	X	X			
Time-Telling Time Lines	F, P	X	X		X	X
Going Graphic: Visual Stories	F, NF, BL	X	X		X	
Press Conferences	F	X	X			X
From Poetry to Plot	F, NF, BL, P	X	X			

Activity ideas are identified as being well-matched for fiction (F), nonfiction (NF), blended (BL), biography (BG) books, and poetry (P).

Supporting Differentiation

All of the book-sharing activities can be used in a variety of ways and lend themselves to the principles of differentiation, supporting students' strengths while also fostering the love of reading. When differentiating instruction, the content (concepts), process (delivery of instruction), and/or the educational product (outcome) can be varied to meet individual student needs. You might note that some activities are especially well suited to being completed by small groups of students. (Look for that designation in the table of contents, page 4.)

To differentiate the content, for example, you might choose to teach the same concept yet use a fiction book with some students, a graphic novel with others, and a nonfiction book with a third group. To differentiate by changing the process during demonstration and guided practice, you may wish to vary the sequence of instructions and/or delivery system by using a PowerPoint presentation or other type of media format such as an audio book. Finally, to differentiate an educational product or outcome, you may wish to guide students to select book-sharing activities that are not only appropriate for their chosen books but that also are suitable for them as individual learners.

Using Picture Books for Modeling

When *Better Than Book Reports* was first printed, using picture books for modeling was a unique approach; however, today using picture books to teach writing and essential reading strategies is common because it has been proven to be so effective, even with upper elementary students. It remains a key component of the teacher-directed Demonstration & Guided Practice sessions. Once students view the demonstration and participate in guided practice for a book-sharing activity, they are prepared to apply this information to a book of their choosing. In this way, students build a repertoire of ways to share books with others. Most important, student-to-student sharing is a powerful way to build and sustain not only reading skills but also the desire to read for pleasure.

How you share a picture book with students is up to you. Some teachers prefer to read the picture book to the whole group during a designated read-aloud time. Others prefer to share and model with small groups over a period of days and then read the book aloud a final time to the entire group before beginning the demonstration and guided practice component. Still other teachers walk around while they read aloud to the whole group and at critical points in the story, stop to show on screen a few pages they have scanned. Decide for yourself which book-sharing activities, teaching methods, and grouping strategies meet your needs and students' needs. And, have fun! You'll keep the classroom a stronghold of literacy-building vibrancy.

Standards Matrix

> Use this matrix in your planning as you select texts and standards on which to focus.

STANDARDS

SUGGESTED ACTIVITIES	BOOK TYPE	WRITING 1	READING 2	SPEAKING AND LISTENING 3	UTILIZING VISUAL/MEDIA LITERACY 4	CONDUCTING RESEARCH/ EXAMINING TEXT IN DETAIL 5
Culture Kits	F, NF, BL	X	X	X		X
Storytelling Tangrams	F		X	X	X	
Story Trees	F, BL	X	X			
A One-Person Show	F, NF, BL	X	X	X		X
Experience the Experiment	F, NF, BL	X	X		X	
Creative Catalogs	F, NF, BL	X	X		X	X
Recipes for Good Books	F, NF, BL	X	X			
Seeing Math	F, NF	X			X	
Fitting the Character to a T	F, NF, BL	X	X			X
Plot Puzzles	F, BL	X	X	X	X	X
All in a Day's Work	NF	X	X		X	X
Two-Person Performances	F, P		X	X		
Story Maps	F, BL	X	X	X	X	X
The What Chart	NF, BL	X	X		X	X
Double-Duty Dictionaries	F, BL	X	X		X	X
Problems and Solutions	F, BL	X	X			
SWBS: A Plot Chart	F	X	X		X	X

Activity	Genre						
Point-of-View Postcards	F, BL	×	×		×	×	×
How-to Lessons	F, NF	×	×	×	×	×	×
A Comparing-Contrasting Map	F, NF, BL	×	×		×	×	×
Crayon Recaps	F	×	×	×	×	×	×
Points-of-Decision Charts	F, BL	×	×		×	×	×
Grouping Books Together	F, NF, BL		×		×	×	×
Sum It Up!	F, NF, BL	×	×				×
Fast-Fact Cards	NF, BL	×	×		×	×	×
Plot Predictions	F	×	×				
Cornering the Conflict	F, BL	×	×		×	×	×
Tell-Along Boards	F	×	×	×	×	×	×
Changing the World: Biographies	BG, BL	×	×		×	×	×
PERSONification Webs	F	×	×		×	×	×
Opinion Pages	F, NF, BL	×	×	×			
Notable Quotables	F, NF, BL	×	×				×
Synonym Strips	F, NF, BL		×		×		×
Thank You Notes	F, NF, BL	×	×			×	
Cause-and-Effect Organizers	F, NF, BL		×		×	×	×
Add-On Stories	F	×	×		×	×	×
Research-Based ABC Books	F, NF	×	×		×	×	×
Words for Wordless Books	F	×	×	×	×	×	×
Pattern Poetry	F, P	×	×	×	×	×	×
Time-Telling Time Lines	F, NF, BL	×	×		×	×	×
Going Graphic: Visual Stories	F	×	×		×	×	×
Press Conferences	NF, BL, BG	×	×	×	×	×	×
From Poetry to Plot	F, NF, BL, P	×	×		×	×	×

Activity ideas are identified as being well-matched for fiction (F), nonfiction (NF), blended (BL), biography (BG) books, and poetry (P).

Culture Kits

The beliefs and behaviors characteristic of a particular people, society, or nation help to define the identity of a culture. For students now well acquainted with instant news and easy-access Internet information, understanding the meaning of "culture" and the role culture plays in our global society is especially important.

Demonstration & Guided Practice

Introduce students to this activity by creating and sharing a Culture Kit based on one of the books listed or based on a book that complements your curriculum. You can create a Culture Kit with your students' participation or you can prepare one ahead of time and present a demonstration. Either way, it's important that you guide students in drawing connections between the book and the cultural artifacts in the kit.

Consider the example of a teacher-created kit based on Ying Chang Compestine's book *Revolution Is Not a Dinner Party* (Holt, 2007). It included flags, chopsticks, and Chinese currency. Following are brief descriptions of the artifacts or items the kit contained and summaries that explain the cultural significance of each item in relation to the book or what those items remind the reader of in terms of a story character's historical context, beliefs about family, traditions, and so on.

ITEM 1: DIFFERENT FLAGS GLUED ONTO THE OUTSIDE OF THE KIT'S BOX

Importance: These flags were used during various periods of China's Communist Revolution and displayed in public places in China, especially during the period in which the main character, Ling, attended school in 1972.

The inside cover of the kit holds a page that explains the significance of each flag.

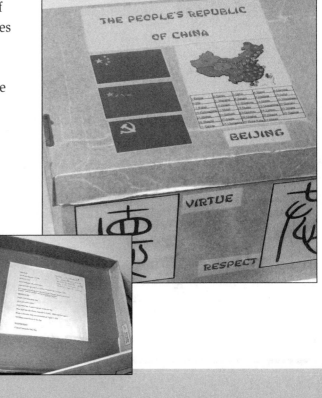

BOOKS FOR MODELING

GRADES 2–4

Are We There Yet? A Journey Around Australia by Alison Lester (Kayne/Miller, 2005)

Prita Goes to India by Prodeepta Das (FrancesLincoln, 2007)

Looking at Ireland by Kathleen Pohl (Gareth Stevens, 2008)

GRADES 4–6

Teens in Brazil by Caryn Garcey Jones (Capstone, 2007)

Horse Song: The Naadam of Mongolia by Ted & Betsy Lewin (Lee & Low, 2008)

Teens in Egypt by Barbara A. Somerville (Capstone, 2007)

FICTION, NONFICTION, AND BLENDED BOOKS WORK BEST WITH THIS ACTIVITY.

TOP FLAG

The People's Republic of China

adopted in 1949

Red is traditional color of revolution

Large gold star represents the Common Program of the Community Partry

Four smaller gold star represent the four classes of people united by the common program: workers, peasants, bourgeois, patriotic capitalists

Yellow was reserved for royal family during ancient dynasties. Yellow now is for everyone — children's caps in yellow

MIDDLE FLAG

People's Liberation Army Flag

red is color of revolution

large golden star is smaller than one on national flag

Three small lines are Chinese numerals for 8 and 1 which stand for August 1

People's Liberation Army was established on August 1, 1928

All Chinese armed forces fly this flag

BOTTOM FLAG

Chinese Communist Party Flag

ITEM 2: FLAT-TIPPED CHOPSTICKS

Importance: Ling's family, the main characters in the book, ate their meager meals with chopsticks.

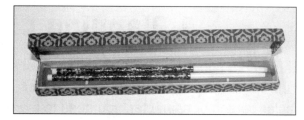

ITEM 3: CHINESE MONEY

Importance: Chinese currency depicts different ethnic groups in China. In this way, the Chinese working class is elevated and is depicted as being loyal to Chairman Mao.

After discussing the process of selecting artifacts of importance to the book, ask students to choose another book to read independently. Distribute copies of Culture Kits: A Planning Checklist (page 12) and Culture Kits: Literature Connections (page 13). Have students use both pages for extra support as they develop their own Culture Kits and then give brief presentations to show what they've learned.

TECHNOLOGY

TIP ➤ Students can find printable maps, flags, and information about different countries at CIA: The World Factbook: Flags of the World: http://www.cia.gov.

NAME _____ DATE _____

CULTURE KITS

A Planning Checklist

To learn about another person's culture, you need to remember that people all over the world have important beliefs and customs. To learn about the culture of a particular person or character, you need to learn what he or she believes about common topics such as family, education, and celebration.

Follow the directions below. Use them as a checklist as you prepare your Culture Kit. After you complete a task, place a check mark in the box to show you followed that step.

•

☐ **1.** Read a fiction or nonfiction book about a family or person from a culture other than your own. Your teacher or school librarian can help you select a book.

☐ **2.** Choose six items, called artifacts, to put into your Culture Kit box. These items must be important to the story or book and represent the culture about which you have learned. You can also create items to place in your kit.

☐ **3.** Complete the Literature Connections page (page 13). On it identify each item or artifact and explain why each is important in the culture you learned about.

☐ **4.** Decorate your Culture Kit box to help show what you've learned about the culture. You can find different images such as flags and photographs on the Internet.

☐ **5.** Prepare to give a presentation to your classmates describing the contents of your Culture Kit. Practice showing each item, describing it, and explaining how it connects to the book you read. Use your completed Literature Connections page to help you. Then place that page in your box so you'll have it to use during your presentation.

Better Than Book Reports © 2009 by Christine Boardman Moen, Scholastic Teaching Resources

CULTURE KITS

Literature Connections

Below, write the name of each item in your Culture Kit and explain why it is important in the culture you've read about.

Book title _____

Author _____

Item 1: _____ It is important because _____

_____

_____

Item 2: _____ It is important because _____

_____

_____

Item 3: _____ It is important because _____

_____

_____

Item 4: _____ It is important because _____

_____

_____

Item 5: _____ It is important because _____

_____

_____

Item 6: _____ It is important because _____

_____

_____

Storytelling Tangrams

Tangrams, ancient Chinese puzzles, are squares that have been cut into seven pieces. Each puzzle piece is called a tan. In this book-sharing activity students use tans to create pictures while telling their story. (Another activity that uses a similar strategy is Crayon Recaps on page 71.)

Demonstration & Guided Practice

During traditional Chinese storytelling, all seven tans of the Tangram puzzle are used to create a picture. The storyteller places the tans so they touch one another without overlapping.

To introduce students to telling stories with tans, you may want to read aloud *Grandfather's Shape Story.* Pause reading to demonstrate how to use the seven tans to create some of the patterns shown in the text. You may find it helpful to draw a puzzle pattern for each animal on tag board. Then, during the reading, you can place the tans onto the puzzle pattern.

To give students hands-on practice working with tans, divide the class into partner groupings. Distribute copies of Storytelling Tangrams: Puzzle Pieces (page 17) so that each student has his or her own set of tans to color, cut out, and manipulate. Have partners take turns arranging the tans and guessing whether the arrangement depicts an animal, object, or person. (For sturdier puzzle pieces, trace and then cut the shapes from construction paper, card stock, or cardboard.)

Next, explain that you will be reading aloud *Where the Wild Things Are.* (Older students will enjoy one of the stories listed for their grade level or a short story.) At the end of the reading, each student will create a scene, character, or object from the story using his or her set of tans. Although in traditional Chinese storytelling, each puzzle must consist of seven tans, allow students to use all seven tans or as few tans as they wish for their puzzles. When students have completed their patterns, have a "gaze and praise walk" or an opportunity for students to view each other's patterns. While each student's puzzle will be different, you'll find a few simple pattern suggestions for *Where the Wild Things Are* on the following page.

After students have demonstrated that they can manipulate the tans for storytelling, ask them to choose books to read independently. After reading, students will then prepare to use their tans in a short retelling of the book they've read. Distribute copies of Storytelling Tangrams: Planning Page (page 16). Explain that students should use their tans and the student page to help them plan and deliver an oral presentation that will in part show what they understand about their book's characters, setting, beginning, middle, and end.

BOOKS FOR MODELING

GRADES 2–4

Grandfather's Shape Story by Brian Sargent (Scholastic, 2007)

Duck and Goose by Tad Hills (Schwartz & Wade, 2006)

Tangram Magician by Lisa Campbell Ernst (Blue Apple Books, 2005)

GRADES 4–6

Grandfather Tang's Story by Ann Tompert (Knopf, 1990)

The Tangram ABC Book by Thomas Foster (BookSurge, 2006)

Iggy Peck, Architect by Andrea Beaty (Abrams Books, 2007)

FICTION BOOKS WORK BEST WITH THIS ACTIVITY.

TECHNOLOGY

TIP ➤ Invite students to practice manipulating tans digitally by visiting http://itangram.tripod.com.

Important object tangrams for *Where the Wild Things Are*

(left) Max's boat (". . . he sailed off through the night and day and in and out of weeks and almost over a year to where the wild things are.")

(right) Max's supper (". . . waiting for him and it was still hot")

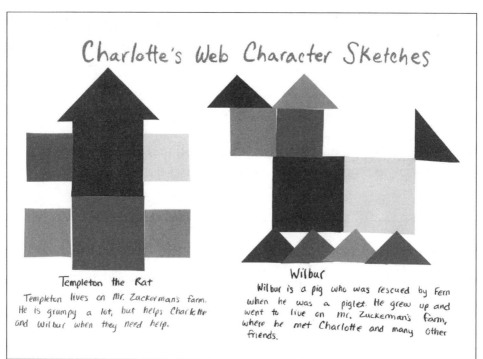

Character tangram puzzles for *Charlotte's Web.*

STORYTELLING TANGRAMS

Planning Page

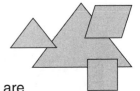

During traditional Chinese storytelling, all seven tans of a Tangram puzzle are used to create a picture. The storyteller places the tans so they touch one another without overlapping. You can tell stories with tans, too. To get started, color and cut out the pieces on Storytelling Tangrams: Puzzle Pieces, page 17.

Follow the directions below, using as many or as few of the tans as you wish to help you plan a storytelling presentation about the book you've read.

Book title _____

Author _____

1. Think about the main character(s) in your story. Use your tans to create a puzzle that looks like or represents the character. Draw your puzzle in the first box.

2. Think about something important that happened to the main character or an important place the character went. Use your tans to make a puzzle that looks like the event or place. Draw your puzzle in the second box.

3. Think about how the story ended. Use your tans to make a puzzle that reminds you of the ending of the book. Draw your puzzle in the third box.

4. If there are any other events, places, or characters you want to include in your presentation, use your tans to make puzzles. Draw them on the back of this page.

5. Next, practice telling about the book you've read and putting together your puzzles. You can use this page as a guide as you practice and during your storytelling presentation.

1

2

3

Better Than Book Reports ©2009 by Christine Boardman Moen, Scholastic Teaching Resources

STORYTELLING TANGRAMS

Puzzle Pieces

Color and cut out the Tangram pieces below. Use them as props during your story retellings.

Story Trees

The Story Tree activity, a variation of Brenda Waldo's Story Pyramid, helps students focus on the basic literary elements of plot, character, and setting while encouraging them to use exact language to share their book with others. Ultimately, students create the tree effect by making eight statements using the exact number of required words.

Demonstration & Guided Practice

To introduce students to a Story Tree, read aloud one of the suggested stories or one of your choosing. Then, as a group, complete a Story Tree that you have copied on a board or on screen. Use the Story Trees: Checklist prompts on page 19 to elicit student responses.

After discussing the tree students created as a group, ask them to choose books to read independently. Students in grades 4–6 may wish to complete this activity using short stories instead of longer books. When the group is ready to start the activity, distribute copies of the checklist and Story Trees: Writing Frame (page 20). Explain that students should follow the directions on their checklist to write a concise description about the book they've read. Some students may enjoy using the support of the writing frame provided, while others may prefer to illustrate and fill in their own versions of the Story Tree.

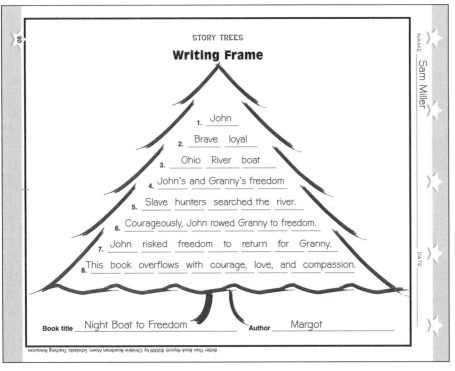

Story Tree for *Night Boat to Freedom*

BOOKS FOR MODELING

GRADES 2–4

Albert the Fix-It Man by Janet Lord (Peachtree, 2008)

Pirate for Hire by Matthew McElligott (Walker, 2007)

I'd Really Like to Eat a Child by Sylviane Donnio (Random House, 2007)

GRADES 4–6

The Boy Who Was Raised by Librarians by Carla Morris (Peachtree, 2007)

Night Boat to Freedom by Margot Theis Raven (Farrar, Straus and Giroux, 2006)

Zen Ties by Jon J. Muth (Scholastic, 2008)

FICTION AND BLENDED BOOKS WORK BEST WITH THIS ACTIVITY.

TECHNOLOGY

TIP ➤ Using a scanned image of the Story Tree along with an LCD projector or interactive whiteboard, you and your students can write, edit, and revise a Story Tree in real time. During revision, it's especially important that students learn the difference between a phrase (a group of words that does not contain a verb) and a sentence (a group of words that contains a subject and predicate and can stand alone and make sense).

STORY TREES

Checklist

A Story Tree cannot be planted; it needs to be built. You can build a Story Tree by following the directions on this page.

After you complete a step in the directions, place a check mark in the box beside it. Do your writing on the allotted lines in the Story Trees: Writing Frame, page 20.

❑ **1.** Write the **name** of the main character in the story.

❑ **2.** Write two **words** that describe the main character.

❑ **3.** Write a three-word **phrase or sentence** that describes where the story takes place (setting).

❑ **4.** Write a four-word **phrase or sentence** telling what the main character wanted in the story.

❑ **5.** Write a five-word **sentence** telling what happened that almost stopped the main character from getting what she or he wanted in the story.

❑ **6.** Write a six-word **sentence** telling how the main character got what she or he wanted in the story.

❑ **7.** Write a seven-word **sentence** that describes the best part of the story.

❑ **8.** Write an eight-word **sentence** telling why you would or would not tell a friend to read this story.

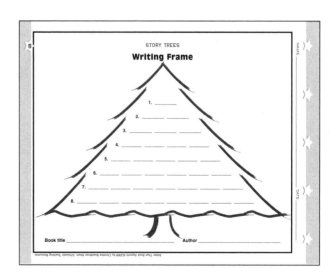

STORY TREES

Writing Frame

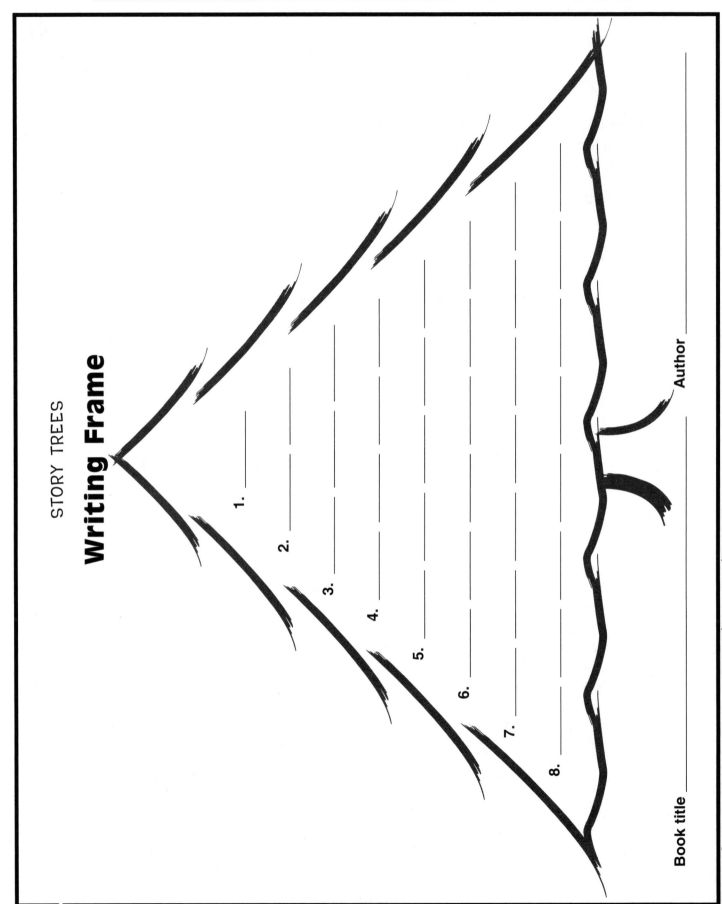

1. _____
2. _____
3. _____
4. _____
5. _____
6. _____
7. _____
8. _____

Author _____

Book title _____

A One-Person Show

Students who enjoy performing will especially enjoy this book-sharing strategy that invites them to tell about a favorite person or character. Each student dresses up in costume to portray that person and, in that guise, talks directly to the audience.

Demonstration & Guided Practice

To help students gain a sense of what is to be expected of them, select a character or person from one of the books listed here or from any book your students may enjoy. Perform your own one-person show for your students or record it and play it for the class. After students observe the performance, read aloud the book in which the character or person appears.

Ask volunteers to make connections between the performance and the story they heard. Discuss the effects of costume, speaking voice, props, and behavior. Next, distribute the One-Person Show: Planning Page (page 22) and go over your expectations for the assignment: Following the planning page instructions, each student will prepare and deliver a performance based on a favorite person or character. Each student should select a book to read independently, complete his or her planning page, and perform a one-person show.

A student portrays Charley Goddard, the main character in Gary Paulsen's *Soldier's Heart* (Laurel Leaf, 2000).

BOOKS FOR MODELING

GRADES 2–4

What to Do About Alice? by Barbara Kerley (Scholastic, 2008)

Manfish: The Story of Jacques Cousteau by Jennifer Berne (Chronicle Books, 2008)

The Silent Witness by Robin Friedman (Houghton Mifflin, 2008)

GRADES 4–6

I, Vivaldi by Janice Shefelman (Eerdmans Books, 2008)

Snow Baby: The Arctic Childhood of Robert E. Peary's Daring Daughter by Katherine Kirkpatrick (Holiday House, 2007)

Lincoln Shot: A President's Life Remembered by Barry Denenberg (Felwel, 2008)

FICTION, NONFICTION, AND BLENDED BOOKS WORK BEST WITH THIS ACTIVITY.

TECHNOLOGY

TIP ➤ Students will likely enjoy a visit to Teacher Tube (www.teachertube.com), which has several videos of people who assume the roles of Abraham Lincoln, Abigail Adams, and other historical figures.

A ONE-PERSON SHOW

Planning Page

To get ready for your one-person performance, read your book and think about the main character. Plan your performance by filling out this sheet. Finally, practice your performance in front of a mirror.

Book title _____

Author _____

Character's name and age _____

1. What will I need to wear in order to show my audience when and where my character lived?

2. How will I need to speak in order to show my character's age? What kind of accent or special words will I need to use? Are there specific words my character is famous for saying?

3. What props will I need? (Props include tables and chairs as well as things actors use like books and reading glasses.)

4. As I pretend to be this character, what will I tell the audience about who my character is, where he or she came from, what he or she thinks and feels, and what has happened in his or her life?

Experience the Experiment

Students are natural "hands-on" learners who want to do things for themselves and see the results of their actions. To combine hands-on learning and literature (fiction and nonfiction), students can "experience the experiment," conducting and observing a simple science experiment that has been featured in a book they've read.

Demonstration & Guided Practice

Introduce an abbreviated form of the Scientific Method by modeling a simple experiment and completing with students Experience the Experiment: Planning Page (page 24). You might want to try the Colored Carnations experiment explained on the Kidzone Web site (see the Technology Tip below) or a simple experiment described in one of the books listed for modeling. As a group, conduct the experiment. Invite volunteers to ask questions about following directions, making predictions, recording observations, and drawing conclusions. For extra practice, student pairs or small groups can conduct different experiments related to everything from plants to popcorn!

When students are ready, distribute copies of the planning page and Experience the Experiment: Process Log (page 25). Explain that each student should select an experiment to conduct from one of the books or Internet resources noted on this page or from another appropriate resource. Students should complete both pages and perform the experiment independently. Later, when they present their findings to the group, they may use the planning page and process log for support.

In this simple experiment white carnations "color" themselves as the stems draw colored water up into the flower.

BOOKS FOR MODELING

GRADES 2–4

What's the Matter in Mr. Whiskers' Room? by Michael Elsohn Ross (Candlewick, 2007)

Science School by Mick Manning (Frances Lincoln, 2008)

Yikes! Wow! Yuck! Fun Experiments for Your First Science Fair by Elizabeth Snoke Harris (Lark Books, 2008)

GRADES 4–6

Galileo's Leaning Tower Experiment by Wendy Macdonald (Charlesbridge, 2009)

Investigating Science: Using Coins, Paper and Rubber Bands by Jan Kaslow (Silverleaf Press, 2008)

Planet Earth: 25 Environmental Projects You Can Build Yourself by Kathleen Reilly (Nomad Press, 2008)

FICTION, NONFICTION, AND BLENDED BOOKS WORK BEST WITH THIS ACTIVITY.

TECHNOLOGY

TIP ➤ Student-friendly science sites include http://kids.yahoo.com/science, which has science videos students can watch; http://www.cool-science-projects.com/elementaryScienceProjects.html and http://www.kidzone.we/science/index.htm, which offer students several easy-to-do experiments.

EXPERIENCE THE EXPERIMENT

Planning Page

This page will help you plan your experiment and think about what you will learn from the results. Read and review this page before, during, and after your experiment.

Title of experiment _____

Book title _____

ASK: What do I want to find out from this experiment?

_____

_____

_____

_____

PREDICT: Your experiment will cause something to happen. What will the cause be? What will the effect be in your experiment? Draw your ideas in the boxes and write a caption for each.

CAUSE	EFFECT

→

_____   _____

_____   _____

_____   _____

_____   _____

EXPERIENCE THE EXPERIMENT

Process Log

LIST: Write the steps you will follow when doing your experiment.

1. _____
2. _____
3. _____
4. _____
5. _____

WATCH: Do the experiment, paying attention to what happens. Record your observations and show what happened in a drawing.

_____

_____

_____

_____

_____

_____

_____

CONCLUDE: What did you learn from your experiment? How was your prediction true or not true?

_____

_____

_____

_____

Creative Catalogs

Many businesses supplement their online offerings with paper catalogs. What catalogs lack in plots and themes, they make up for in their clever use of design and description. For tech-savvy students, using a computer to help create a catalog based on items that are important to fiction or nonfiction characters is an ideal way to combine research, writing, and art or graphic design.

Demonstration & Guided Practice

To begin, bring in catalogs from home or print out some pages from digital catalogs on the Internet. Read aloud about some products so students can become familiar with the word choice and persuasive writing used in catalogs. As a group, discuss how products are displayed and described.

Next, select one of the books listed here or another book that fits with your curriculum. Read aloud a portion of the text and invite volunteers to point out items that the characters used or needed. Explain that students will finish reading the book and select an item for which to write a catalog advertisement. Distribute copies of Creative Catalogs: Ad (page 28). Students who plan to write and illustrate several ads will need multiple copies of the reproducible student page.

You can divide the class into small groups or invite students to write their catalog entries independently. (For some books or products, additional research may be required to help determine pricing and other details.) When students are done writing and revising their ads on their student pages, consider making a collaborative class catalog to showcase student work. Have students cut and paste with scissors and glue, use word-processing software, or access Web ware (see tip).

The next page shows a sample catalog item related to the story *Buffalo Music*, based on the lives of Charles and Mary Ann Goodnight who settled in West Texas in 1876. The text describes how Mary used hot-water bottles and flannel blankets to rescue abandoned buffalo calves. Since the modern-day hot water bottle wasn't created until 1903, a description for a hot water bottle from an 1876 catalog might resemble this one.

BOOKS FOR MODELING

GRADES 2–4

Finding Daddy: A Story of the Great Depression by Jo Harper (Turtle Books, 2005)

Tuttle's Red Barn by Richard Michelson (Putnam, 2007)

Miss Bridie Chose a Shovel by Leslie Connor (Houghton Mifflin, 2004)

GRADES 4–6

Whale Port by Mark Foster (Houghton Mifflin, 2007)

Buffalo Music by Tracey E. Fern (Clarion Books, 2008)

Girl on the High-Diving Horse by Linda Oatman High (Puffin, 2005)

FICTION, NONFICTION, AND BLENDED BOOKS WORK BEST WITH THIS ACTIVITY.

TECHNOLOGY

TIP ➤ Interested in having your students develop a Web page as a class catalog? If you have a g-mail account (or don't mind opening one), just select the Sites category on the Google Product page to get started.

HOT WATER BOTTLE

Keep warm whenever the weather turns cold! These round easy-to-fill hot water bottles keep water hot for hours and hours. Secure stoppers prevent leaks. Choose from earthenware or metal. Approximate size is twelve inches in diameter. For additional cold-weather items, see bed warmers. Order today! Price includes shipping costs!

Price ___$1.00___

Book title ___Buffalo Music___

Author ___Tracey E. Fern___

Your name: ___Jonathan___

Catalog ad for *Buffalo Music*

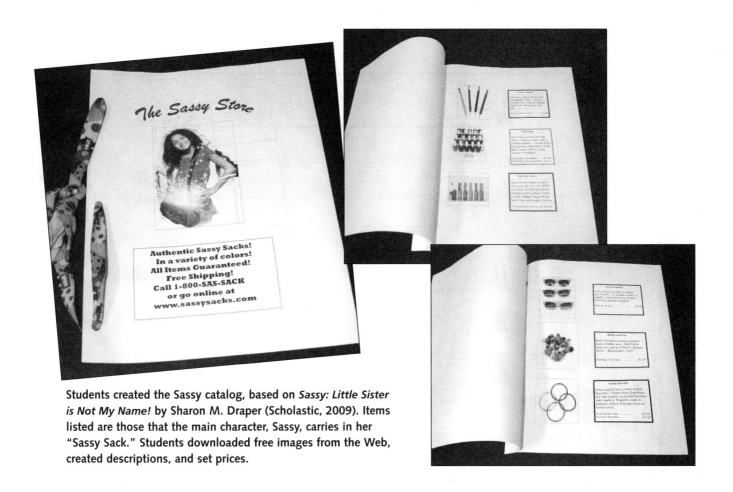

Students created the Sassy catalog, based on *Sassy: Little Sister is Not My Name!* by Sharon M. Draper (Scholastic, 2009). Items listed are those that the main character, Sassy, carries in her "Sassy Sack." Students downloaded free images from the Web, created descriptions, and set prices.

CREATIVE CATALOGS

Ad

Create your own catalog advertisement! To create an effective ad, follow these steps:

1. Select an item that was important during the time period in which the story you read takes place. Learn as much as you can about the item from your reading or do additional research.

2. In the open ad space, draw the item you want to sell. Your picture will help catalog readers see the product.

3. Below the box, write the name of the item.

4. On the lines, tell exciting reasons why someone should buy the item. Use details from your book or research to describe it and ask a reasonable price.

5. Look over your work. What could you do to improve the description or the drawing? Make revisions that will help sell your product.

_____

_____
_____
_____
_____
_____
_____

Price _____

Book title _____

Author _____

Your name: _____

Recipes for Good Books

A story's basic elements of plot, theme, setting, mood, and character-ization become ingredients for student learning with this book-sharing strategy that invites students to create a "literary recipe."

Demonstration & Guided Practice

Help familiarize students with recipes by photocopying a few of your favorite recipes or copying them onto large index cards. As a group, talk about the ways in which a baker or chef uses recipes to create a dish. Explain that in this activity students will develop recipes. Instead of using food they'll be using literary elements (including plot, theme, set-ting, mood, and characterization).

Read aloud one of the books listed here or another book that "mixes in" with your curriculum. After reading, invite volunteers to identify the literary elements of the book. Then, on a board or screen, copy the writing frame as it appears on Recipes for Good Books: Recipe Card (page 30). Ask students to collaborate in writing a recipe with you that highlights the literary elements of the book you shared.

After you've guided students through the process and recorded stu-dents' recipe ideas, explain that students will be using the same strategy to write their own recipes about books they'll select and read independ-ently. For example, after reading Tomie dePaola's *Strega Nona* (Aladdin, 1979), a student's recipe card might resemble the one pictured below.

To extend this activity, have students work cooperatively to create a class recipe book. Divide the class into small groups and then divide up the work with different groups designing the front and back covers, the copyright page, table of contents, index, and so on.

BOOKS FOR MODELING

GRADES 2–4

Dear Mr. Rosenwald by Carole Boston Weatherford (Scholastic, 2006)

Help Me, Mr. Mutt!: Expert Answers for Dogs With People Problems by Janet Stevens and Susan Stevens Cummel (Harcourt, 2008)

When Ruby Tried to Grow Candy by Valorie Risher (Schwartz & Wade, 2008)

GRADES 4–6

The Girl in the Castle Inside the Museum by Kate Bernheimer (Schwartz & Wade, 2008)

The Pink Refrigerator by Tim Egan (Houghton Mifflin, 2007)

Hey Batta Batta Swing!: The Wild Old Days of Baseball by Sally Cook and James Charlton (Margaret K. McElderry, 2007)

FICTION, NONFICTION, AND BLENDED BOOKS WORK BEST WITH THIS ACTIVITY.

From the kitchen of ___Cecelia___
(student's name)

Boil together one plot that ___has a magic pasta pot. It boils out of control and almost destroys the whole town.___

Mix in characters, including ___a friendly witch named Strega Nona who has a helper, Big Anthony. He doesn't pay attention to the whole magic chant. Then he tries to show off.___

Place it in ___the town of Calabria in Italy___

Sprinkle with feelings of ___fun and worry___

Garnish with a message about ___disobeying and punishing people fairly. Big Anthony has to eat all the pasta!___

Book title ___Strega Nona___

Author ___Tomie dePaola___

Illustrator ___Tomie dePaola___

TECHNOLOGY

TIP ➤ This book-sharing activity is much like an abbreviated book review. To give students more experience reading conventional book reviews online, consider visiting Miami University's database of children's picture books at http://www.lib.muohio.edu/pictbks/.

RECIPES FOR GOOD BOOKS

Recipe Card

Use the recipe card below to describe a book that's "good enough to eat"! These are the recipe ingredients (the story's literary elements) that you'll need to include:

Plot: what happened

Character(s): the names of the main characters and some words that describe them (friendly, mean, funny, etc.)

Setting: where it happened

Mood: the main feeling (calm, scary, silly, etc.)

Theme: the main message or idea

From the kitchen of _____

(student's name)

Boil together one plot that _____

_____

Mix in characters, including _____

_____

Place it in _____

Sprinkle with feelings of _____

Garnish with a message about _____

Book title _____

Author _____

Illustrator _____

Seeing Math

Students connect math and literature in meaningful ways with this book-sharing activity that invites them to "see" how math impacts a story-book's message and applies to real-life situations.

Demonstration & Guided Practice

Introduce students to this activity by reading aloud one of the books listed or another story that complements your math curriculum. After reading, discuss the ways in which mathematics appears in the text. As a group, use details from the story to create math-related problems, charts, and graphs.

For example, after reading Dyanne Disalvo-Ryan's *Uncle Willie and the Soup Kitchen* (HarperTrophy, 1997), tell students to pretend they will be helping at a soup kitchen every day for a week. Their job is to count the number of people who come to the kitchen each day and to create a line graph showing the sum.

Next, open a regular-size loaf of bread and let students count the number of slices. (Most regular-size loaves have about 20 slices, including the two crusts.) Have students calculate the number of loaves the kitchen would have used each day if every person ate two pieces of bread per day. Finally, have students create a bar graph to reflect the number of loaves eaten during one week and ask each other questions based on the graph's information (see the example on page 32).

When students have demonstrated understanding about connections between math and literature, distribute copies of Seeing Math: Problems and Answers (page 33). Explain that students will be creating their own math problems and answers about books they'll select. You can have students work independently, in pairs, or small groups.

Students who excel at math may enjoy taking this activity further. After they've completed their problems and answers pages, ask students to copy their math problems onto index cards. Have students exchange cards with partners or within groups. When everyone has solved all of the problems, have each student tell his or her partner or group how the math problem connects to the selected book.

BOOKS FOR MODELING

GRADES 2–4

Mummy Math: An Adventure in Geometry by Cindy Neuschwander (Square Fish, 2009)

Isabel's Car Wash by Sheila Bair (Albert Whitman, 2008)

The Lion's Share: A Tale of Halving Cake and Eating it, Too by Matthew McElligott (Walker, 2009)

GRADES 4–6

Using Math in the ER by Hilary Koll, Steve Mills, & Dr. Kerrie Whitwell (Gareth Stevens, 2007)

The Wishing Club: A Story About Fractions by Donna Jo Napoli (Henry Holt, 2007)

Sir Cumference and the Isle of Immeter by Cindy Neuschwander (Charlesbridge Publishing, 2006)

FICTION AND NONFICTION BOOKS WORK BEST WITH THIS ACTIVITY.

TECHNOLOGY

TIP ➤ WebQuests are a fun way to practice math skills. Check out Teacher Tap at http://annettelamb.com/tap/topic4/htm, which lists numerous engaging WebQuests and http://www1.smd.org/staffdev/elementary/web_quests.htm, Interactive Web Sites PK–6.

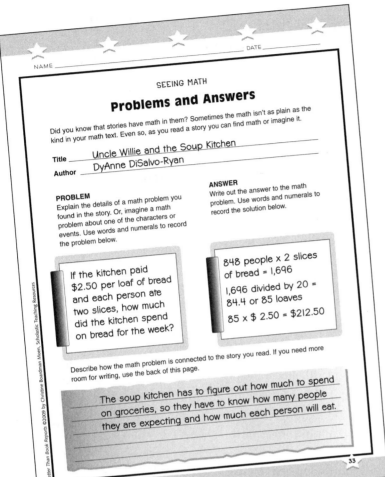

SEEING MATH

Problems and Answers

Did you know that stories have math in them? Sometimes the math isn't as plain as the kind in your math text. Even so, as you read a story you can find math or imagine it.

Title _Uncle Willie and the Soup Kitchen_

Author _DyAnne DiSalvo-Ryan_

PROBLEM
Explain the details of a math problem you found in the story. Or, imagine a math problem about one of the characters or events. Use words and numerals to record the problem below.

If the kitchen paid $2.50 per loaf of bread and each person ate two slices, how much did the kitchen spend on bread for the week?

ANSWER
Write out the answer to the math problem. Use words and numerals to record the solution below.

848 people x 2 slices of bread = 1,696

1,696 divided by 20 = 84.4 or 85 loaves

85 x $ 2.50 = $212.50

Describe how the math problem is connected to the story you read. If you need more room for writing, use the back of this page.

The soup kitchen has to figure out how much to spend on groceries, so they have to know how many people they are expecting and how much each person will eat.

Better Than Book Reports ©2009 by Christine Boardman Moen, Scholastic Teaching Resources

33

Students use story details to create and solve math problems. They can support and extend their understanding with a visual representation, such as a bar graph.

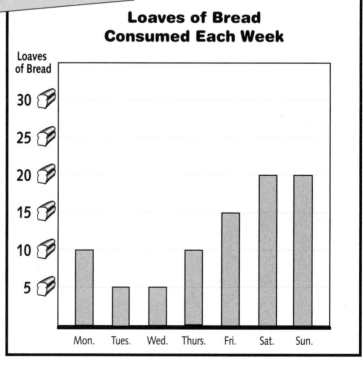

Loaves of Bread Consumed Each Week

Loaves of Bread graph with values 5, 10, 15, 20, 25, 30 on the y-axis and Mon., Tues., Wed., Thurs., Fri., Sat., Sun. on the x-axis.

SEEING MATH

Problems and Answers

Did you know that stories have math in them? Sometimes the math isn't as plain as the kind in your math text. Even so, as you read a story you can find math or imagine it.

Title _____

Author _____

PROBLEM

Explain the details of a math problem you found in the story. Or, imagine a math problem about one of the characters or events. Use words and numerals to record the problem below.

ANSWER

Write out the answer to the math problem. Use words and numerals to record the solution below.

Describe how the math problem is connected to the story you read. If you need more room for writing, use the back of this page.

_____
_____
_____
_____
_____

Fitting the Character to a T

Some book characters demand a reader's attention. Junie B. Jones and Stanley Yelnats from Louis Sachar's book *Holes* are characters that readers pay attention to because they are interesting. When the idea of character is a book's theme, this activity can help students zero in on personality traits and better grasp the concept of character.

Demonstration & Guided Practice

After reading aloud one of the books listed here or another of your choosing, ask students to describe what they know about the main character and what they know about the kind of person the main character is. Use a board or screen to record volunteers' answers on a T-chart. On the left side of the chart, record a particular character's traits or characteristics. Write examples that support these traits on the right. Guide students to use specific examples from the text to support their conclusions, as shown on the following page in the example from *Sarah, Plain and Tall* (Harper & Row, 1985).

Once students have completed a T-chart with you and have demonstrated their understanding of the activity, explain that they should select a longer book to read and complete a T-chart. Distribute the student page Fitting the Character to a T (page 36). (You can have them work independently, in partners, or in small groups.)

Take this activity a step further by dividing the class into small groups and assigning each group a different character from the same book. When students have completed their T-charts, ask each group to share its findings with the class. When the sharing is done and the evidence presented, invite students to share any additional insights they may have about a particular character or characters.

BOOKS FOR MODELING

GRADES 2–4

The Firekeeper's Son by Linda Sue Park (Clarion, 2004)

Louis Sockalexis: Native American Baseball Pioneer by Bill Wise (Lee & Low, 2007)

Glamsters by Elizabeth Cody Kimmel (Hyperion, 2008)

GRADES 4–6

Different Like Coco by Elizabeth Matthews (Candlewick, 2007)

At Gleason's Gym by Ted Lewin (Roaring Brook Press, 2007)

Strong to the Hoop by John Coy (Lee & Low Books, 1999)

FICTION, NONFICTION, AND BLENDED BOOKS WORK BEST WITH THIS ACTIVITY.

TECHNOLOGY

TIP ➤ Through publishing-house Web sites, many authors have pages where they share what inspired their writing and even what inspired them to develop certain characters. Here are a few publishing Web site URLs you might share with students: Lee & Low at http://www.leeandlow.com, Scholastic at www.Scholastic.com, and Hyperion at http://www.hyperionbooksforchildren.com.

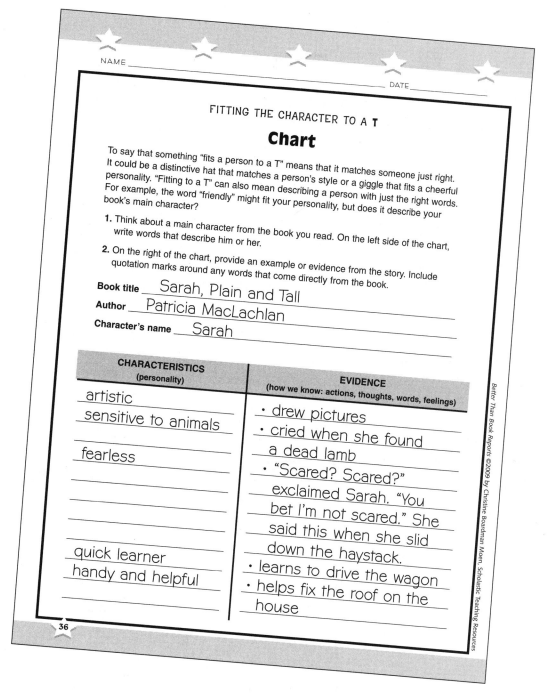

NAME _____ DATE _____

FITTING THE CHARACTER TO A **T**

Chart

To say that something "fits a person to a T" means that it matches someone just right. It could be a distinctive hat that matches a person's style or a giggle that fits a cheerful personality. "Fitting to a T" can also mean describing a person with just the right words. For example, the word "friendly" might fit your personality, but does it describe your book's main character?

1. Think about a main character from the book you read. On the left side of the chart, write words that describe him or her.

2. On the right of the chart, provide an example or evidence from the story. Include quotation marks around any words that come directly from the book.

Book title _Sarah, Plain and Tall_

Author _Patricia MacLachlan_

Character's name _Sarah_

CHARACTERISTICS (personality)	EVIDENCE (how we know: actions, thoughts, words, feelings)
artistic	• drew pictures
sensitive to animals	• cried when she found a dead lamb
fearless	• "Scared? Scared?" exclaimed Sarah. "You bet I'm not scared." She said this when she slid down the haystack.
quick learner	• learns to drive the wagon
handy and helpful	• helps fix the roof on the house

Better Than Book Reports ©2009 by Christine Boardman Moen, Scholastic Teaching Resources

Character traits for Sarah supported by evidence from the book

FITTING THE CHARACTER TO A **T**

Chart

To say that something "fits a person to a T" means that it matches someone just right. It could be a distinctive hat that matches a person's style or a giggle that fits a cheerful personality. "Fitting to a T" can also mean describing a person with just the right words. For example, the word "friendly" might fit your personality, but does it describe your book's main character?

1. Think about a main character from the book you read. On the left side of the chart, write words that describe him or her.

2. On the right of the chart, provide an example or evidence from the story. Include quotation marks around any words that come directly from the book.

Book title _____

Author _____

Character's name _____

CHARACTERISTICS (personality)	EVIDENCE (how we know: actions, thoughts, words, feelings)

Plot Puzzles

Many readers visualize a story they're reading, imagining scene after scene as the plot unfolds. This activity taps into that visualization strategy and enables every reader to participate in summarizing a story line and depicting favorite scenes.

Demonstration
& Guided Practice

Before beginning this activity in the classroom, select a book to share with the group. Make a copy of Story Summary (page 41) and complete it with drawings of your favorite scenes and a brief summary of the story. Leave your page intact, as you'll turn it into a puzzle later.

Read the book aloud to the group. Then show students the page you completed before the session. Take time to examine the scenes you've drawn and to share your brief story summary. Ask volunteers to tell whether they would have chosen the same scenes and share why or why not.

Tell students that you need their help in turning the story summary page into a puzzle. Turn the page over so it faces down. Invite a volunteer to draw five or six interlocking jigsaw pieces and then cut the page apart into those puzzle pieces. Invite another volunteer to reassemble the puzzle.

BOOKS FOR MODELING

GRADES 2–4

Sergio Makes a Splash! by Edel Rodriguez (Little, Brown, 2008)

Never Take a Shark to the Dentist by Judi Barrett (Atheneum, 2008)

The Cow That Laid an Egg by Andy Cutbill (HarperCollins, 2008)

GRADES 4–6

Armando and the Blue Tarp School by Edith Hope Fine & Judith Pinkerton Josephson (Lee & Low, 2007)

Phillis's Big Test by Catherine Clinton (Houghton Mifflin, 2008)

Frankenstein Takes the Cake by Adam Rex (Harcourt, 2008)

FICTION AND BLENDED BOOKS WORK BEST WITH THIS ACTIVITY.

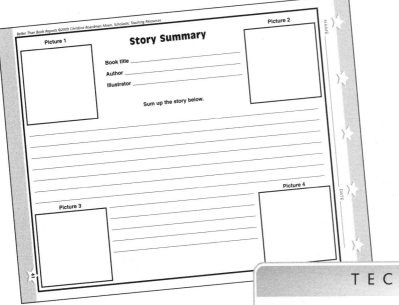

TECHNOLOGY

TIP ➤ Some students will enjoy the drawing component in this activity. Other students may prefer to use free Clip Art from Florida's Educational Technology Clearinghouse, http://etc.usf.edu/clipart/. The site offers more than 38,000 images to choose from.

Select a book for the whole class to read and give every student a copy of Story Summary. You'll need to provide students working independently with copies of Plot Puzzles: Checklist A (page 39) and students working with a partner or group with copies of Plot Puzzles: Checklist B (page 40). Students should follow the directions on their checklists to complete this activity. You may want to have younger students and strong visual learners select and draw the four most important scenes first, discuss them with a partner, and then create the summary based on their images and discussion.

When the puzzles are complete, store them in self-sealing storage bags. (Hint: Laminate the puzzles or have students mount them on card stock for durability.) Students should trade bags with their peers, giving everyone an opportunity to put together a different puzzle and discuss the summaries and talk about why some students chose one favorite scene over another.

Picture 1   Picture 2

Book title The Twin Princes.
Author Tedd Arnold.
Illustrator Tedd Arnold.

Tell about the story: The Story is about twin chickens. The King had two sons and he hardly Knew them. The King had to Pick the next King. The two brothers raced. Henry the sweet Son. became King when he won the race.

Name Gina.

Picture 3   Picture 4

Students' responses are illustrated with four key events. The next step is to cut the page into puzzle pieces and swap puzzles with a partner. Partners reconstruct and then enjoy their classmate's plot summary.

Picture 1   Picture 2

Book title Henry's Freedom box
Author Ellen Levine
Illustrator Kadir Nelson

Tell about the story: Henry mails him self to Pennsylvainia. So that he can find freedom. But first he must travel there. So his friends help him. He packs him-self in a wooden crate and travels to Philadelphia. I like this book because a slave travels in America for his freedom.

Name Stephanie

Picture 3   Picture 4

PLOT PUZZLES

Checklist A

Follow the directions below. Use them as a checklist as you prepare your
Story Summary on page 41 and make your puzzle. After you complete a task,
place a check mark in the box to show you followed that step

☐ **1.** After reading, consider what the book is about. Sum up the story in a few sentences.

☐ **2.** Record your ideas on the Story Summary.

☐ **3.** Reread what you wrote and make any corrections.

☐ **4.** Decide what four events or scenes are your favorites.

☐ **5.** Show those events in the corner boxes of Story Summary. You may illustrate the
scenes or use another method your teacher approves.

☐ **6.** Turn the Story Summary page over. Using a pencil, draw a jigsaw puzzle pattern of
five or six pieces. Label each piece with your name.

☐ **7.** Cut out the puzzle pieces. When you're done, write your name on a self-sealing bag
and put your puzzle pieces inside.

☐ **8.** Trade bags with a partner and put his or her puzzle together. Read the book
summary and look at the favorite scenes. Talk about why his or her Story Summary
page has similar or different information or images than your page.

☐ **9.** Trade bags with another partner until you have put together three puzzles.

☐ **10.** On the back of this page, share your observations about your partners' Story
Summary pages. What did you have in common with them? In what ways did your
Story Summary differ from theirs?

PLOT PUZZLES

Checklist B

Follow the directions below. Use them as a checklist as you prepare your Story Summary on page 41 and make your puzzle. After you complete a task, place a check mark in the box to show you followed that step.

☐ **1.** After reading, discuss what the book is about. Sum up the story in a few sentences.

☐ **2.** Take turns writing the summary.

☐ **3.** Take turns reading what you wrote and make any corrections.

☐ **4.** Decide what four events or scenes are your favorites.

☐ **5.** Take turns showing scenes in the corner boxes of Story Summary. You may illustrate the scenes or use another method your teacher approves.

☐ **6.** Turn the Story Summary page over. Using a pencil, draw a jigsaw puzzle pattern of five or six pieces. Label each piece with all the names of group members.

☐ **7.** Take turns cutting out the puzzle pieces. When you're done, write your names on a self-sealing bag and put your group's puzzle pieces inside.

☐ **8.** Trade bags with another group and put their puzzle together. Read the book summary and look at their favorite scenes. Talk about how their Story Summary page contains similar or different information from your group's page.

☐ **9.** Trade bags with another group until your group has put together all the other groups' puzzles.

Better Than Book Reports © 2009 by Christine Boardman Moen, Scholastic Teaching Resources

NAME ______________________ DATE ______________

Picture 1

Story Summary

Picture 2

Book title ______________________

Author ______________________

Illustrator ______________________

Sum up the story below.

____

____

____

____

____

____

____

Picture 3

____

____

____

____

____

Picture 4

All in a Day's Work

The world of work is of high interest to children, who enjoy thinking about what they're going to be when they grow up. This book-sharing activity draws on that interest and helps strengthen students' sequencing skills as they explore what a person does typically in "a day's work."

Demonstration & Guided Practice

Read aloud one of the books listed here or a book of your choice that features an interesting occupation or profession. To help excite younger students who may enjoy learning what you do as a classroom teacher, prepare a simple PowerPoint presentation of photos of activities you do during your daily schedule. Older students might enjoy *Career Ideas for Kids Who Like Sports* by Diane Lindsey Reeves (Checkmark Books, 2007). As a broad introduction to careers, choose *When I Grow Up: A Young Person's Guide to Interesting and Unusual Occupations* by Jessica Loy (Holt, 2008). Alternatively, read poems from Tracie Vaughn's *Steady Hands: Poems About Work* (Clarion, 2009).

After reading about and discussing different occupations and professions with the group, have students select a book to read on the topic. Copy All in a Day's Work (page 43) on the board or display it on screen. Invite volunteers to draw as well as tell what a worker does throughout a typical day. As a group, discuss the sequence of tasks as well as the related skills and responsibilities.

To take this book-sharing activity further, ask students to select books to read independently, in partners, or in small groups. Distribute copies of All in a Day's Work and have students record what they've learned about a typical day in one particular occupation or profession. Let students use drawings in the boxes to scaffold their writing.

BOOKS FOR MODELING

GRADES 2–4

Dinosaur Hunters: Paleontologists by Richard Spilsbury (Heinemann, 2007)

Forest Firefighters by William David Thomas (Gareth Stevens, 2008)

Mountain Rescuer by William David Thomas (Gareth Stevens, 2008)

GRADES 4–6

ER Vets: Life in an Animal Emergency Room by Donna M. Jackson (Houghton Mifflin, 2005)

Be a Volcanologist by Suzy Gaslay (Gareth Stevens, 2008)

Video Game Designer by Kevin Cunningham (Cherry Lake, 2009)

NONFICTION BOOKS WORK BEST WITH THIS ACTIVITY.

A sixth-grader records the three-part day of a stained-glass artist in a word-processing program and creates a piece of artwork to pair with the description.

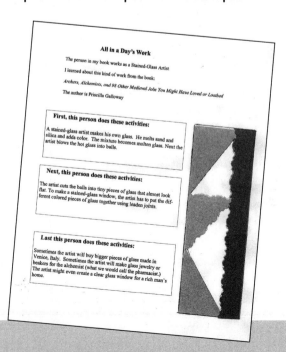

TECHNOLOGY

TIP ➤ Have students produce and narrate their own PowerPoint presentations using the student page All in a Day's Work as a framework. Students ready to conduct additional research about occupations can check out http://www.kids.gov. The site not only has links to other content areas, but also describes occupations and careers all the way from A to Z with "A Day in the Life of a Special Agent" to "Working at the San Diego Zoo."

All in a Day's Work

Using the book you read for reference,
answer the questions below.

The person in my book works as a(n) _____ .

I learned about this kind of work from the book: _____

_____ .

The author is _____ .

In the boxes, draw or tell what the person in your book does when he or she works.

First, this person does these activities:

[ ]

Next, this person does these activities:

[ ]

Last, this person does these activities:

[ ]

On the back of this page, draw a picture that shows why this person's job is important.

Two-Person Performances

Using this book-sharing strategy, two people present a piece of literature in a modified version of a choral reading. Student pairs select an appropriate piece of literature, create a script, practice, and perform the piece for an audience.

Demonstration & Guided Practice

If you are unfamiliar with poetry performance, then a first step might be to read Sara Holbrook's *Wham! It's a Poetry Jam* (Boyds Mill, 2002). It offers simple, practical advice describing how to help students perform, not just read, poetry. Another way to introduce students to Two-Person Performance is to give a performance with the help of a colleague. A fellow teacher, librarian, or school media specialist could help you perform "Book Lice" or "Water Boatmen" from *Joyful Noise: Poems for Two Voices* or "Copycats" from Holbrook's book. Older students also may enjoy a read-aloud of Brod Bagart's *Hormone Jungle: Coming of Age in Middle School* (Maupin House, 2006).

Younger students may already be familiar with Mary Ann Hoberman's books. Before having students perform, read aloud one or two of Hoberman's stories. An alternative is to read aloud Steven Layne's *Love the Baby,* and let the entire class chime in on the line "Love the baby." An additional story that allows the entire class to chime in during a read-aloud is Susan Meyers' *Kittens! Kittens! Kittens!* (Abrams, 2007). When students hear you read aloud the repetitive line "Here and there and everywhere!," students chime in with "kittens, kittens, kittens!"

After your performance, show students a copy of the Two-Person Performances Checklist (page 45). Explain that pairs of students will use that page for support as they select a poem or a book that "reads like poetry," mark their parts, practice the reading several times, and then perform the poem or story for the class.

BOOKS FOR MODELING

GRADES 2–4

You Read to Me, I'll Read to You: Very Short Scary Tales to Read Together by Mary Ann Hoberman (Little, Brown, 2007)

You Read to Me, I'll Read to You: Very Short Stories to Read Together by Mary Ann Hoberman (Little, Brown, 2006)

Love the Baby by Steven L. Layne (Pelican, 2007)

GRADES 4–6

Joyful Noise: Poems for Two Voices by Paul Fleischman (HarperTrophy, 2004)

This Is Just to Say: Poems of Apology and Forgiveness by Joyce Sidman (Houghton Mifflin, 2007)

Birds on a Wire by J. Patrick Lewis and Paul B. Janeczko (Boyds Mills, 2008)

FICTION BOOKS AND POETRY WORK BEST WITH THIS ACTIVITY.

Students rehearse for their retelling of a folktale.

TECHNOLOGY

TIP ➤ Youth Radio often has podcasts of students performing their original two-person poems. The site can be found at http://youthradio.wordpress.com. If you would like to create performances for podcasting, check out the information at the Education Podcast Network at http://wpnweb.org/. Alternatively, you can record your own performances on DVD.

NAME _____ DATE _____

PARTNER'S NAME _____

TWO-PERSON PERFORMANCES

Checklist

Use this checklist to help you and your partner prepare for your Two-Person Performance. Select a piece of literature to perform. Record the title and author below.

Title _____

Author _____

Which statement best describes how you've divided the piece? Check one.

❑   We have found a poem or story that can be divided into two parts so it sounds like a conversation.

❑   We have found a poem or story that can be divided into two parts with one person telling the story and the other person talking to the audience and making comments about the story.

❑   We have found another way of dividing the poem or story into two different parts. (Use the back of this page to describe how you have divided it.)

1. Prepare the script. Check off the steps you have followed.

❑   Decide who will read which lines. Read the story or poem aloud to see if the way you've divided it up makes sense.

❑   Word process the scripts so that each performer has a copy with double spacing between lines.

❑   To prevent the paper from making rattling noises during the performance, tape the script copies onto heavy card stock.

❑   Color-code your lines by highlighting each performer's part in a different color.

2. Practice for the performance. Check off the steps you have followed.

❑   Plan any gestures or body movements you want to include in the performance and mark them in the script.

❑   Record your performance so that you can later evaluate it.

❑   Review your performance. Identify areas that need improvement (i.e., tone, speed, gestures).

❑   Practice your performance until you feel ready to perform it for an audience.

Story Maps

When students use maps to find their way through the plot of a story, geography becomes more than a list of names and places. This book-sharing activity is designed to help students develop the visual literacy skill of map reading as well as learning other map-related concepts such as scale and direction.

Demonstration
& Guided Practice

Begin this activity by reading aloud Uri Shulevitz's poignant book *How I Learned Geography* (Farrar, Straus and Giroux, 2008). This brief auto-biography, which is appropriate for students in grades 2–6, celebrates how a poor refugee escapes the poverty and hardships of his circum-stances through imaginative journeys with a colorful map. An alternate approach to this subject is to share *Maps and Mapping* by Jinny Johnson (Kingfisher, 2007). It describes a variety of map types, from relief maps to political maps to physical maps, and covers topics from continents to countries. One final way is to share Loreen Leedy's wonderful book *Mapping Penny's World*, which is bound to inspire the most reluctant student of geography.

While reading one of the suggested books, pause from time to time to demonstrate in what ways the story lends itself to mapping. Use a copy of the U.S.A. Map (page 49) or another map as a prop to plot a route of travel. Talk about how the story takes place in a setting, events occur at different landmarks, characters travel by boat across rivers, and so on. Invite volunteers to assist you in the process of identifying impor-tant places and plotting them on a map.

After reading, tell students that they should select a book to read that lends itself to a mapping activity. Fiction books or blended books in which the characters travel work well for this activity. You might say, for example, that one student might select a fictional story about a solitary adventurer, while another might choose a blended book in which a famous statesman takes his family on a journey across a sea.

BOOKS FOR MODELING

GRADES 2–4

The Great White House Breakout by Helen Thomas and Chip Bok (Dial, 2008)

Americana Adventure by Michael Garland (Dutton, 2008)

Off We Go to Mexico by Laurie Krebs (Barefoot Books, 2008)

GRADES 4–6

Close to the Wind: The Beaufort Scale by Peter Malone (Putnam, 2007)

Go, Go, America by Dan Yaccarino (Scholastic, 2008)

The Magic Baseball Cap by David A. Ham and Janice B. Sibley (CRM, 2006)

FICTION AND BLENDED BOOKS WORK BEST WITH THIS ACTIVITY.

TECHNOLOGY

TIP ➤ In addition to viewing detailed maps on the Internet, students are also able to get a satellite image and view a country's terrain by going to http://maps.google.com and typing in a country's name. If you can navigate through the advertise-ments, http://www.webcrawler.com offers free printable maps.

Explain that students will read their selections and then prepare their own maps that help describe the plot of the book they've read. Distribute copies of Story Maps: Planning Page (page 48). Explain that students should use this page to help them show what they understand about their book's characters, setting, beginning, middle, and end. When possible students should identify key landmarks described in the book (monuments, cities, rivers). In some cases, students will need to draw their own original maps. In other instances students will be able to use the reproducible U.S.A. Map provided on page 49 or use another outline map downloaded from the Internet. (See the Technology Tip.)

Students can layer their Story Maps with illustrations or text boxes to highlight key events and settings along the route. Here a student uses settings and objects central to Sal's and her mother's journeys in *Walk Two Moons* by Sharon Creech (HarperCollins, 1994).

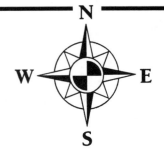

STORY MAPS

Planning Page

You will create a map that shares information about a main character and his or her travels.

Book title _____

Author _____

Character's name _____

1. While reading, use sticky notes to flag the parts that tell where the main character is located at the start of the story, where he or she goes, and where he or she ends up.

2. Draw the character's route on a map.

   • If you can use a map of the United States, ask your teacher for a copy of page 49.

   • If the character travels to another country or countries, get the reproducible outline maps you'll need from your teacher, the Internet, or alternate resource.

3. Mark the important places the main character visits or stays at while traveling along the trail.

   • How are cities, mountains, rivers, and lakes shown? (Look at a map key for help.)

   • What details can I add to help show where an event took place?

   • Have I labeled important places?

4. Share your map or maps with your classmates. Explain the beginning, middle, and end of your character's route. Describe why the places you marked are important.

STORY MAPS

U.S.A. Map

Route of _____ in the book _____ by _____

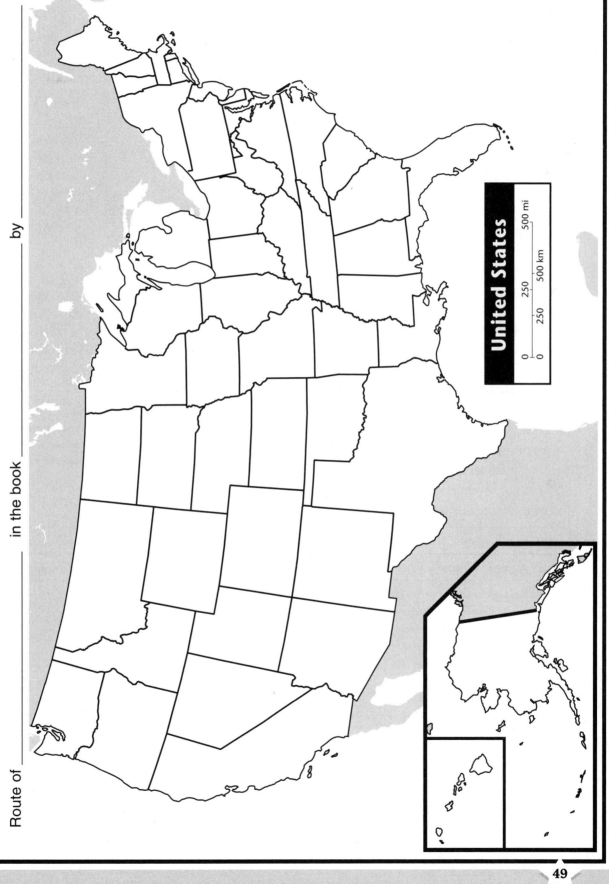

United States

500 mi

250

500 km

0   250

0

The What Chart

This book-sharing activity, a variation of a KWL chart, requires students to tap into their prior knowledge about a particular topic, plan individual purposes for reading, and evaluate what they've read. The What Chart helps students organize these tasks. The "What" in the chart's name stands for *What* I Know Already, *What* I Want to Know, and *What* I've Learned from Reading.

Demonstration & Guided Practice

Work with students to fill in the chart before, during, and after you read aloud one of the books suggested here or after they have read a book of their choice.

Many children think of technology today in terms of the Internet, cell phones, and gaming systems. You can challenge that notion and introduce this book-sharing activity by reading *Mr. Lincoln's High-tech War*. (Allow ample time as the text is lengthy.) The information in Allen's book may help students rethink the term "high-tech" as they discover that Lincoln pushed the Northern states to the cutting edge of technology during the American Civil War. He provided the leadership necessary to design ironclad warships, develop a new type of rifle, and even use hot-air balloons for surveillance.

Duplicate the What Chart (page 51) on the board or on screen and work with students to complete the chart. On the board, you can use sticky notes or sentence strips to move information from one column to the next as students learn and/or confirm information or as more questions arise.

BOOKS FOR MODELING

GRADES 2–4

Clarabelle: Making Milk and So Much More by Cris Peterson (Boyds Mills, 2007)

Abe's Honest Words: The Life of Abraham Lincoln by Doreen Rappaport (Hyperion, 2008)

Spiders by Nic Bishop (Scholastic, 2007)

GRADES 4–6

Military Dogs by Frances Ruffin (Bearport, 2006)

The Mysterious Universe by Ellen Jackson (Houghton Mifflin, 2008)

Mr. Lincoln's High-tech War by Thomas B. Allen (National Geographic, 2009)

NONFICTION AND BLENDED BOOKS WORK BEST WITH THIS ACTIVITY.

Title: Mr. Lincoln's High-Tech War   **Author:** Thomas B. Allen & Roger MacBride Allen

WHAT I ALREADY KNOW	WHAT I WANT TO KNOW	WHAT I'VE LEARNED FROM READING
Lincoln was president during the Civil War. Lincoln was killed while he was still president. Lincoln delivered the Gettysburg Address. Lincoln put Grant in charge of the Union army. There is a statue of Lincoln in Washington, D.C.	What does "high-tech" mean in the title of the book? What new inventions did Lincoln support during the war? Did these high-tech innovations help the North win the war?	Lincoln supported the production and use of the Spencer Repeating Rifle. This weapon gave the Union troops "a deadly and decisive advantage." (p. 96) Lincoln had the *Monitor* built. Three things were unique about this ship. 1. It was an ironclad, so it had iron plating to protect it. 2. The ship was propeller-driven and didn't need sails. 3. It had a gun turret that allowed it to shoot iron balls in several directions while the ship maneuvered. "The *Monitor* is the proud ancestor of them all [today's combat ships]." (p. 65) Lincoln supported a Union aeronaut: Thaddeus Lowe. He flew in an observation balloon to give the army accurate information about battles and troop movements. Aeronauts even spied at night on encampments to estimate troop numbers. Lowe helped save the Union army from destruction at the Battle of Fair Oaks because of his "frequent and accurate reports." (p. 48)

TECHNOLOGY

TIP ➤ To differentiate this activity, set up an interactive report page using Google Docs. By selecting the Simple Report template, students can add, revise, and delete information in real time and have a finished collaborative report of their combined What Charts. Go to http://google.com and type in Google Docs. Note that you must have a g-mail account to use Google Docs. The account is free and easy to set up.

The What Chart

Use this chart before, during, and after you read to learn about your topic or story. Follow the directions and record information below.

1. Choose a book on a topic that interests you.

Book title _____

Topic _____   **Author** _____

2. Before you read your book, think about what you already know about the topic. Write your ideas on the chart under "What I Know Already."

3. Think about what you want to learn about the topic. Write your ideas on the chart under "What I Want to Know."

4. While reading your book and after reading your book, think about what you've learned. Write these ideas on the chart under "What I've Learned From Reading."

What I Know Already	? What I Want to Know ?	What I've Learned From Reading

Double-Duty Dictionaries

A Double-Duty Dictionary is a student-created dictionary that lists words in English as well as in another language. It demonstrates usage either by using the word correctly in a sentence or illustrating it with a simple drawing.

Demonstration & Guided Practice

Read aloud from one of the books listed here or another book of your choosing. After reading, assist students in selecting three words to include in the dictionary. You might, for example, point out places in the text where an author has inserted words from another language followed by a phrase or group of words that explains the unfamiliar word. Or, you might invite volunteers to point out non-English words and explain their meaning from their context within the story.

Divide the class into small groups. Provide each group with a copy of the Double-Duty Dictionaries: Definition Page (page 55). Have students in each group take turns drawing illustrations and writing sentences to accompany the three dictionary words you worked with them to identify earlier in the lesson. Then have groups show their work and explain their entries to the class. This is an opportunity for students to review the target words multiple times in the context of memorable examples from their peers.

When students are ready, explain that each student should choose a book to read independently. Distribute copies of the Planning Page (page 54) and the definition page. Following the directions on the planning page, students should create a dictionary page. Have English language learners first list the words in their native language, then English, and finally in the language used in the book. Ask students to return to their small groups to share and discuss their dictionary entries. Finally, gather student pages into a binder and place it in the classroom library. You can build on it later and use the collaborative dictionary as a classroom resource.

Double-Duty Dictionaries can be easily created using word processing software that creates tables for words, definitions, and sentences. For example, students may wish to create a dual-language dictionary that uses sentences taken from the text. The first example shown here is an excerpt from a student-created dictionary based on Susan Middleton Elya's *Oh No, Gotta Go!* (Putnam, 2003). Once their

BOOKS FOR MODELING

GRADES 2–4

Yatandou by Gloria Whelan (Sleeping Bear Press, 2007)

The Butter Man by Elizabeth Alalou (Charlesbridge, 2008)

For You Are a Kenyan Child by Kelly Cunnane (Simon & Schuster, 2006)

GRADES 4–6

The Best Eid Ever by Asma Mobin-Uddin (Boyds Mills, 2007)

Martina the Beautiful Cockroach retold by Carment Agra Deedy (Peachtree, 2007)

Hiromi's Hands by Lynne Barasch (Lee & Low, 2004)

FICTION AND BLENDED BOOKS WORK BEST WITH THIS ACTIVITY.

TECHNOLOGY

TIP ➤ Use PowerPoint to create a presentation of the sentences from the text that contain non-English words and their English appositives. Type the non-English words in italics and their appositives in uppercase letters. Explain that some authors use appositives to help readers understand unfamiliar words.

dictionaries are completed, students use the dictionary for repeated reading practice by reading the sentences and repeating the Spanish words and their English translations.

In the second example, a student uses illustrations to provide the definitions for the foreign words she has encountered in *Yatandou*. Additionally, she makes an editorial note speculating about the words' origins. Have students who are ready for a challenge engage in some basic etymological research and consider the types of editorial notes they might add to their dictionaries.

Spanish Word	English Translation	Sentence From Text
azul	blue	"Then look for the restaurant, the blue one—azul."
baño	bathroom	"Where is un (the) baño?"
camino	street or highway	"We were out driving, down the camino."

Double-Duty Dictionary

Yatandou by Gloria Whelan and Peter Sylvada

A Special Note About This Dictionary

The story in *Yatandou* takes place in the African country of Mali. French is the official language of Mali, but 80 percent of the people speak a language called Bambara. The book doesn't say what language is used, but I checked and the words used in this dictionary are not French. I think the words may be Bambara, but I'm not sure.
The Editor

English Word	Word from Story	Definition or Example
Scarf	Hawli	
Skirt	Pagne	
Pants	Bantalons	
Wandering Storyteller and Singer	Griot	

This example, created in a word-processing program and then illustrated by hand, includes an editorial note that brings up a question about the language and culture represented in the book.

DOUBLE-DUTY DICTIONARIES

Planning Page

A Double-Duty Dictionary has a lot in common with the dictionaries you've used. First, words are listed alphabetically. Words are defined or explained. Some words have small drawings or illustrations next to them to help explain the words. Finally, words are sometimes used in sentences to explain their meaning.

　　　Use a copy of the Definition Page (page 55) and follow the directions below to make your own dictionary page. It will be different from regular dictionary pages because it will list words both in English and another language.

1. Read a book that has words or expressions in a language other than English.

2. Look for three non-English words you'd like to have in your dictionary. Use bookmarks or sticky notes to keep track of where you found them.

3. In alphabetical order, list the English translation.

4. In the middle column, write the non-English words that match.

5. In the example column, use the non-English word in a sentence or add a picture that shows the word's meaning.

　　• Your sentence should have correct spelling and punctuation.

　　• Your picture should be a drawing, magazine clipping, or piece of clip art.

DOUBLE-DUTY DICTIONARIES

Definition Page

Book title _____

Author _____

English	Other Language	Example

Problems and Solutions

This book-sharing activity encourages students to practice and apply their critical thinking and problem-solving skills as they read narrative text.

Demonstration & Guided Practice

Read aloud one of the books listed here or one that complements your curriculum. After the reading, distribute copies of Problems and Solutions (page 57) and explain that students will use the page as a guide for discussion and a place to record their ideas.

You can have the class discuss the book together or organize students in small discussion groups. Students should focus on identifying the problem or conflict in the story and how the conflict was resolved. Next, have students provide suggestions for alternative solutions to the problem.

Alternately, divide the class into groups and have each group read a different book, discuss the book's primary conflict, and work collaboratively to complete a student page. Ask a volunteer from each group to share the group's observations with the class. Or, invite each group to perform scenes that illustrate the story's problem, solution, and possible alternative solutions.

BOOKS FOR MODELING

GRADES 2–4

Keep Your Ear on the Ball by Genevieve Petrillo (Tilbury House, 2007)

If a Chicken Stayed for Supper by Carrie Weston (Holiday House, 2007)

Henry and the Buccaneer Bunnies by Carolyn Crimi (Candlewick, 2005)

GRADES 4–6

Four Feet, Two Sandals by Karen William and Khadra Mohammed (Erdmans, 2007)

The Impossible Patriotism Project by Linda Skeers (Dial, 2007)

My Chincoteague Pony by Susan Jeffers (Hyperion, 2008)

FICTION AND BLENDED BOOKS WORK BEST WITH THIS ACTIVITY.

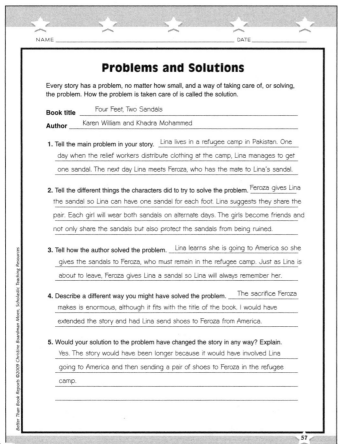

NAME _____ DATE _____

Problems and Solutions

Every story has a problem, no matter how small, and a way of taking care of, or solving, the problem. How the problem is taken care of is called the solution.

Book title _____ Four Feet, Two Sandals _____

Author _____ Karen William and Khadra Mohammed _____

1. Tell the main problem in your story. Lina lives in a refugee camp in Pakistan. One day when the relief workers distribute clothing at the camp, Lina manages to get one sandal. The next day Lina meets Feroza, who has the mate to Lina's sandal.

2. Tell the different things the characters did to try to solve the problem. Feroza gives Lina the sandal so Lina can have one sandal for each foot. Lina suggests they share the pair. Each girl will wear both sandals on alternate days. The girls become friends and not only share the sandals but also protect the sandals from being ruined.

3. Tell how the author solved the problem. Lina learns she is going to America so she gives the sandals to Feroza, who must remain in the refugee camp. Just as Lina is about to leave, Feroza gives Lina a sandal so Lina will always remember her.

4. Describe a different way you might have solved the problem. The sacrifice Feroza makes is enormous, although it fits with the title of the book. I would have extended the story and had Lina send shoes to Feroza from America.

5. Would your solution to the problem have changed the story in any way? Explain. Yes. The story would have been longer because it would have involved Lina going to America and then sending a pair of shoes to Feroza in the refugee camp.

Better Than Book Reports ©2009 Christine Boardman Moen, Scholastic Teaching Resources

57

TECHNOLOGY

TIP ➤ Ask students to show their alternative solutions by drawing a cartoon strip on the board or on screen. Have volunteers show their cartoons and discuss how their alternative solutions address the primary conflict in the story.

? Problems and Solutions

Every story has a problem, no matter how small, and a way of taking care of, or solving, the problem. How the problem is taken care of is called the solution.

Book title _____

Author _____

1. Tell the main problem in your story. _____

_____

_____

2. Tell the different things the characters did to try to solve the problem. _____

_____

_____

_____

3. Tell how the author solved the problem. _____

_____

_____

4. Describe a different way you might have solved the problem. _____

_____

_____

5. Would your solution to the problem have changed the story in any way? Explain.

_____

_____

_____

_____

SWBS: A Plot Chart

SWBS: The Plot Chart is a quick and easy way to check students' comprehension. Since its development by Barbara Schmidt of California State University at Sacramento, this activity has been used with success by an increasing number of teachers and reading specialists.

Demonstration & Guided Practice

Display SWBS: A Plot Chart (page 60) on a board or screen. Discuss what each letter in the abbreviation represents: SWBS stands for SOMEBODY (the main character), WANTED (the character's motivation), BUT (the problem), SO (the solution).

Before reading aloud from one of the books listed here or another book that complements your curriculum, remind students to pay attention to the following:

- the character who is SOMEBODY

- the thing that character WANTED

- the problem he or she experienced (BUT)

- the way the problem was solved (SO)

The easy-to-remember format reads "*Somebody* [name of character], *wanted* to [goal], *but* [problem], *so* [solution]."

Model how each piece of information should be written in the columns of the SWBS chart. Alternately, you can have students illustrate the answers. For example, if you have read aloud *Madeline's Rescue* by Ludwig Bemelmans (Viking Press, 1953) a student might draw Madeline, Miss Clavel, and eleven girls to show S for SOMEBODY and Madeline clutching Genevieve, the dog who rescued her, to show the W for WANTED. The drawings can serve as a scaffold to writing. (See the examples.)

After the closing of the story, discuss the story's ending. Note that in some instances, as in life itself, problems are not neatly solved but people and characters often learn from their experiences, and this is a resolution in itself.

When students have demonstrated that they understand how to identify parts of the story and fill in the chart, distribute copies of the plot chart. Explain that each student should select a book to read independently and complete a SWBS chart based on his or her book.

BOOKS FOR MODELING

GRADES 2–4

For the Love of Autumn by Patricia Polacco (Philomel, 2008)

Moo Who by Margie Palatini (HarperTrophy, 2007)

Knuffle Bunny Too: A Case of Mistaken Identity by Mo Willems (Hyperion, 2007)

GRADES 4–6

Two Bobbies by Kirby Larson and Marty Nethery (Walker, 2008)

Pale Male: Citizen Hawk of New York City by Janet Shulman (Knopf, 2008)

Pitching in for Eubie by Jerdine Nolen (Amistad, 2007)

FICTION BOOKS WORK BEST WITH THIS ACTIVITY.

TECHNOLOGY

TIP ➤ Books on CD or audiotape are readily available at public libraries and may be available at your school's library. Invite small groups of students to listen to and discuss a story, then work together to complete a SWBS chart.

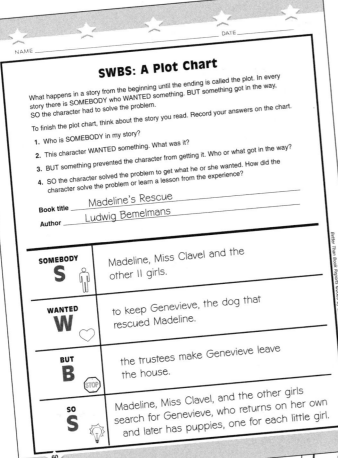

SWBS: A Plot Chart

What happens in a story from the beginning until the ending is called the plot. In every story there is SOMEBODY who WANTED something. BUT something got in the way, SO the character had to solve the problem.

To finish the plot chart, think about the story you read. Record your answers on the chart.

1. Who is SOMEBODY in my story?

2. This character WANTED something. What was it?

3. BUT something prevented the character from getting it. Who or what got in the way?

4. SO the character solved the problem to get what he or she wanted. How did the character solve the problem or learn a lesson from the experience?

Book title _____ Madeline's Rescue

Author _____ Ludwig Bemelmans

SOMEBODY S	Madeline, Miss Clavel and the other 11 girls.
BUT B STOP	the trustees make Genevieve leave the house.
SO S	Madeline, Miss Clavel, and the other girls search for Genevieve, who returns on her own and later has puppies, one for each little girl.

Class plot chart for *Madeline's Rescue*

Younger students may wish to draw their response on the plot chart.

SWBS: A Plot Chart

What happens in a story from the beginning until the ending is called the plot. In every story there is SOMEBODY who WANTED something. BUT something got in the way, SO the character had to solve the problem.

To finish the plot chart, think about the story you read. Record your answers on the chart.

1. Who is SOMEBODY in my story?

2. This character WANTED something. What was it?

3. BUT something prevented the character from getting it. Who or what got in the way?

4. SO the character solved the problem to get what he or she wanted. How did the character solve the problem or learn a lesson from the experience?

Book title _____

Author _____

SWBS: A Plot Chart

What happens in a story from the beginning until the ending is called the plot. In every story there is SOMEBODY who WANTED something. BUT something got in the way, SO the character had to solve the problem.

To finish the plot chart, think about the story you read. Record your answers on the chart.

1. Who is SOMEBODY in my story?

2. This character WANTED something. What was it?

3. BUT something prevented the character from getting it. Who or what got in the way?

4. SO the character solved the problem to get what he or she wanted. How did the character solve the problem or learn a lesson from the experience?

Book title _____

Author _____

SOMEBODY S	
WANTED W	
BUT B STOP	
SO S	

Point-of-View Postcards

Although many people today tell others of their travels by e-mailing messages, photographs, and sending e-cards, many people still mail postcards, which are actually mini-picture stories. This book-sharing activity uses postcards to support students' understanding of plot, setting, theme, and characterization.

Demonstration & Guided Practice

Select a story to read. Scan or make a transparency of the Point-of-View Postcards Template (page 64). You will use this with students after sharing the read-aloud.

Begin the demonstration and guided practice session by showing students several different paper postcards and creating a list of their common attributes. For example, most postcards have a picture on the front, a brief explanation of the picture on the back of the card, and places for a message, address, and a stamp. Show students the template on screen and invite volunteers to identify the parts of the postcard and how one might use a copy of the page to make a postcard for mailing.

After the read-aloud, invite volunteers to help write a collaborative class postcard. You might begin by having a student draw on the front of the postcard a picture that shows where the main character is located (the setting) at the beginning of the story or during a favorite scene in the story. Next, invite volunteers to help you compose a brief note from the perspective (point of view) of one of the characters in the story. Discuss how the message briefly describes an experience (a plot point) and gives clues about how the character is feeling (tone). Remind the group that the correspondence and illustration go hand in hand. When the writing is complete, review the postcard the group has created. Invite volunteers to describe ways to improve it and meet the goal of writing from the perspective of a character. Make any necessary adjustments to the model postcard.

Distribute copies of the student pages, the Point-of-View Postcards Planning Page (page 63) and the Template. Have each student create a postcard about the book you've read aloud. Once the postcards are complete, divide the class into small groups. Have students exchange and read each other's postcards.

Another approach to this activity for older students and/or for those students who are learning to conduct research is to share Robert Burleigh's *American Moments* (Holt, 2004). Students pretend they are witnesses or participants of such historic events as George Washington crossing the Delaware, watching

BOOKS FOR MODELING

GRADES 2–4

Off We Go to Mexico by Laurie Krebs (Barefoot Books, 2008)

Pictures From Our Vacation by Lynne Rae Perkins (Greenwillow, 2007)

Carl's Summer Vacation by Alexandra Day (Farrar, Straus and Giroux, 2008)

GRADES 4–6

A Couple of Boys Have the Best Week Ever by Maria Frazee (Harcourt, 2008)

Turtle Summer: A Journal for My Daughter by Mary Alice Monroe (Sylvan Dell, 2007)

Happy Tails: The Call of Nature by Cindy and Kirby Pringle (Dogtown Artworks, 2008)

FICTION AND NONFICTION BOOKS WORK BEST WITH THIS ACTIVITY.

TECHNOLOGY

TIP ➤ Students of all learning styles will likely enjoy creating and composing postcards online. The URL that follows is for a student-friendly site that provides templates for teachers and their students: http://www.readwritethink.org/materials/postcard.

the Wright brothers' first flight, or stepping on the moon with Neil Armstrong. After reading the brief description of the event in Burleigh's book, students research the historical event and create a first-person postcard.

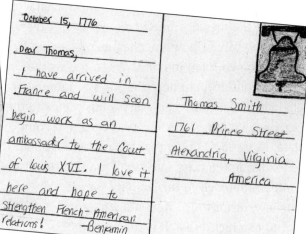

Postcards following Benjamin Franklin's travels

POINT-OF-VIEW POSTCARDS

Planning Page

People look at a postcard's picture and read its message to learn where its sender has been and what he or she has been doing.

After reading your book, follow these directions to create a postcard.

1. Imagine you are one of the characters in the book. Think about what your postcard's picture will look like and what information the message will contain.

2. Decide what place or scene from the story you will draw. Draw it on the front of the postcard.

3. On the back of the card, name the place you've drawn and record the title and author of the book.

4. On the back of the card, write the postcard's message as if you are the character in the book.

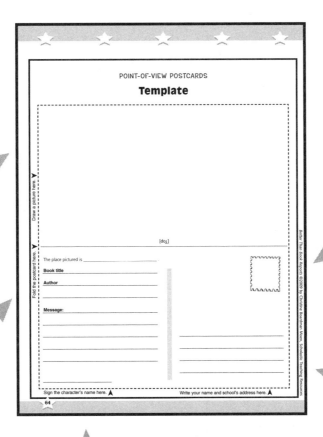

5. Write your name and the school's address on the back of the card. Or address the postcard to another character from the book.

6. Draw a stamp where a stamp should go.

7. Cut out the postcard along the dotted lines, fold it in half, and tape or glue the blank sides together.

POINT-OF-VIEW POSTCARDS

Template

Draw a picture here. ►

Fold the postcard here. ►

[Top]

The place pictured is _____ .

Book title _____

Author _____

_____

Message: _____

_____

_____

_____

_____

_____

_____

_____

_____

Sign the character's name here. ▲

Write your name and school's address here. ▲

How-to Lessons

Students love to demonstrate and talk about what they excel at, and this book-sharing strategy takes advantage of that enthusiasm. Not only does this activity ask students to plan and organize a how-to lesson for their peers, it also challenges them to use information from their reading to show their classmates how to build or create something following a sequence.

Demonstration & Guided Practice

To introduce students to this activity you can first read H. A. and Margret Rey's book *Curious George Rides a Bike* (Houghton Mifflin, 2006) and then demonstrate how to make a paper boat.

Read aloud the story and pause when you reach the part of the story where George makes boats out of the newspapers he is supposed to be delivering. Explain that you need students' help to teach a how-to lesson on making paper boats and that you will use the book's instructions for support. Invite volunteers to help you organize and gather classroom materials for making paper boats. Copy the How-to Lessons Planning Page (page 67) on the board or display it on screen. Have volunteers help you think of the steps a person should follow to plan the demonstration and then complete a boat. Encourage volunteers to make predictions about what problems may occur during the demonstration and suggest ways to anticipate and avoid problems. Finally, have students join you in following the book's instructions for making paper boats. After everyone has folded a newspaper boat, finish reading the story.

Divide the class into small groups, or pairs, or have students read a book independently. Explain that students will read the book and select a simple procedure to demonstrate that is related to an event or object described in the book. Make sure students' ideas are simple enough to describe in three to six steps and have them complete a planning page, and give a how-to lesson to their classmates. Distribute copies of the planning page for students to use during the planning process and as support during the demonstration. Provide students with ample time and opportunities to practice and gain confidence conducting their lessons prior to their whole-group demonstration.

To provide students with more pictorial support, read aloud a high-interest photo-based informative narrative, such as Ulli Steltzer's fascinating book *Building an Igloo* (Holt, 1999), which depicts a father-and-son team building an igloo. While sharing the story, have students complete their planning pages. Invite students to review the text and its photographs for information and planning ideas. If necessary, require students to engage in additional research.

BOOKS FOR MODELING

GRADES 2–4

My Dadima Wears a Sari by Kashmira Sheth (Peachtree, 2007)

May I Pet Your Dog? by Stephanie Calmenson (Clarion Books, 2007)

Origami Master by Nathaniel Lachenmeyer (Albert Whitman, 2008)

GRADES 4–6

Let's Go Geocaching by John McKinney (DK Publishing, 2008)

How to Survive in Antarctica by Lucy Jane Bledsoe (Holiday House, 2006)

How Soccer Works by Keltie Thomas (Maple Tree Press, 2007)

FICTION AND NONFICTION BOOKS WORK BEST WITH THIS ACTIVITY.

TECHNOLOGY

TIP ➤ Have students read and follow directions for creating everything from paper airplanes to cooking zucchini at http://www.howstuffworks.com.

NAME _____ DATE _____

HOW-TO LESSONS

Planning Page

After you've read your book, use the chart below to plan a lesson on how to build or create something.

Book title _____

Author _____

What you will teach	Materials you will need	Problems that might occur	Possible solutions
How to make a paper cup	8-inch square sheet of paper	One sloppy fold can create problems	Add hint to Step 1.

In order, describe the steps you will follow during your how-to lesson. The first three steps have been labeled for you. Use the back of this page for writing and drawing the rest of the steps.

Step 1. Begin with an 8-inch square sheet of paper. Fold the paper diagonally to make a triangle. <u>HINT:</u> Be sure to line up the edges exactly so the next steps will be easy to fold.

Step 2. Fold one corner of the triangle until the point meets the opposite side. <u>HINT:</u> Make your creases sharp!

Step 3. Fold down the first layer of the small triangle at the top. Tuck this piece into the pocket of the cup as far as it will go. Crease the fold.

STEP 4

Flip over the paper and repeat steps 2 and 3, folding up the bottom corner and folding down and tucking in the top triangle.

STEP 5

Gently press the sides to open the cup.

STEP 6

Fill with treats!

The planning page helps students organize their steps, both in writing and in pictures (digital photos were cut out and pasted on this form). This can serve as a scaffold for informative narrative (how-to) essay writing.

HOW-TO LESSONS

Planning Page

After you've read your book, use the chart below to plan a lesson on how to build or create something.

Book title _____

Author _____

What you will teach	Materials you will need	Problems that might occur	Possible solutions

In order, describe the steps you will follow during your how-to lesson. The first three steps have been labeled for you. Use the back of this page for writing and drawing the rest of the steps.

Step 1.

Step 2.

Step 3.

A Comparing-Contrasting Map

The graphic organizer in this book-sharing activity works in much the same way as a Venn diagram, which shows how two things are alike and different. A Comparing-Contrasting Map invites readers to compare and contrast information from within the same book or two different books.

Demonstration
& Guided Practice

You can use this strategy in a variety of ways with both fiction and non-fiction books. For instance, you can have students compare and contrast characters within the same book or from two different books. Or students can compare and contrast characters and settings from books with the same theme or different books written by the same author.

For example, in a unit of study about Native Americans, you might choose to contrast two books written as retellings of folktales, such as *The Mud Pony* and *The Girl Who Loved Horses*. You might read the books aloud or read one aloud and have students read the other in small groups. As a class or in small groups, ask students to compare and contrast elements of the books, including the characters' backgrounds, the setting, the relationship of the characters to nature, and the artwork. Scan or make a transparency of the Comparing-Contrasting Map (page 70) and display it on screen. As a group complete the map (see the example on the next page.)

Distribute copies of the map to students. Students who are especially able readers and enjoy reading may want to read a pair of books that can be compared and contrasted, and then complete the chart themselves. Or, you may wish to have students select a partner for this activity. For instance, two students may wish to read two sports-themed books written by the same author and compare and contrast the main characters or the problem. Other student pairs may want to compare and contrast the text structures or information presented in two nonfiction books written on a topic of interest.

BOOKS FOR MODELING

GRADES 2–4

The Girl Who Loved Wild Horses by Paul Goble (Atheneum, 2001)

The Mud Pony by Caron Lee Cohen (Scholastic, 1989)

Wild Horses: Galloping Through Time by Kelly Milner Halls (Darby Creek, 2008)

GRADES 4–6

Ida B. Wells: Let the Truth Be Told by Walter Dean Myers (Amistad, 2008)

Yours for Justice, Ida B. Wells: The Daring Life of a Crusading Journalist by Phillip Dray (Peachtree, 2008)

Ida B. Wells-Barnett: Strike a Blow Against Glaring Evil by Anne E. Schraff (Enslow Publishing, 2008)

FICTION, NONFICTION, AND BLENDED BOOKS WORK BEST WITH THIS ACTIVITY.

TECHNOLOGY

TIP ➤ Comparing and contrasting is really about evaluating information. Using the Internet, have students compare and contrast different schools' Web site home pages. This is a safe and fun activity that allows students to view and evaluate information schools have in common.

Better Than Book Reports ©2009 by Christine Boardman Moen, Scholastic Teaching Resources

A Comparing-Contrasting Map

Whenever you tell how things are alike, you are comparing them. Whenever you tell how things are different, you are contrasting them. Below is a Comparing-Contrasting Map that you can complete and share with classmates.

1. Write the names of the two things you are comparing and contrasting in the circles under the words "Different."

2. Write the differences near the lines coming out of the circles.

3. Write how the two things are alike on the lines under "Alike."

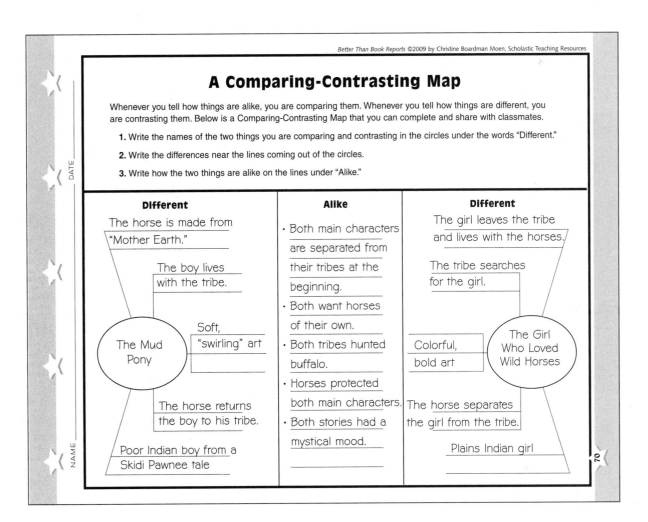

Different

The horse is made from "Mother Earth."

The boy lives with the tribe.

Soft, "swirling" art

The Mud Pony

The horse returns the boy to his tribe.

Poor Indian boy from a Skidi Pawnee tale

Alike

- Both main characters are separated from their tribes at the beginning.
- Both want horses of their own.
- Both tribes hunted buffalo.
- Horses protected both main characters.
- Both stories had a mystical mood.

Different

The girl leaves the tribe and lives with the horses.

The tribe searches for the girl.

Colorful, bold art

The Girl Who Loved Wild Horses

The horse separates the girl from the tribe.

Plains Indian girl

DATE

NAME

70

A Comparing-Contrasting Map

Whenever you tell how things are alike, you are comparing them. Whenever you tell how things are different, you are contrasting them. Below is a Comparing-Contrasting Map that you can complete and share with classmates.

1. Write the names of the two things you are comparing and contrasting in the circles under the words "Different."
2. Write the differences near the lines coming out of the circles.
3. Write how the two things are alike on the lines under "Alike."

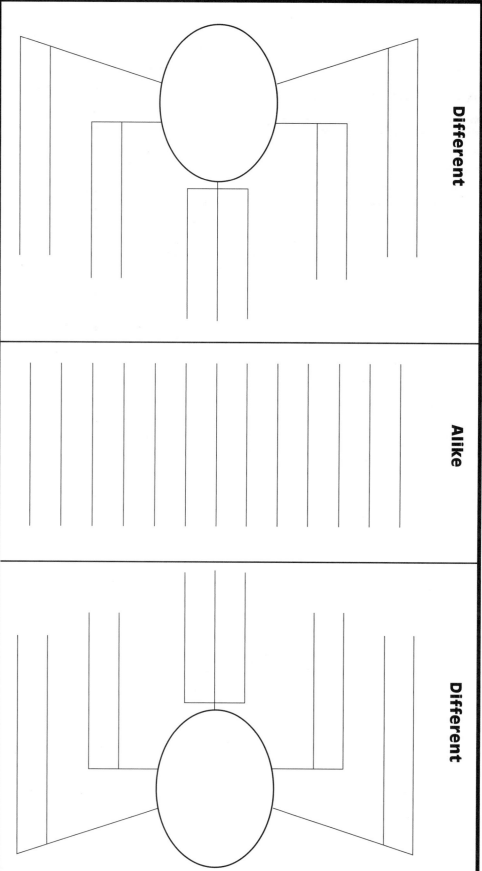

Different

Alike

Different

Better Than Book Reports ©2009 by Christine Boardman Moen, Scholastic Teaching Resources

Crayon Recaps

The Crayon Recaps book-sharing activity is a blend of art and story-telling. Your student storytellers will use crayons and markers (or other means) to portray the adventure they encountered in their reading.

Demonstration & Guided Practice

Introduce the activity by reading aloud Crockett Johnson's classic book *Harold and the Purple Crayon* (HarperTrophy, 1998), making sure that students are able to see the simple line drawings. Ask students to explain how Harold's drawings help tell the story as it unfolds.

Choose one of the stories listed above and read it aloud *without* showing students the illustrations. Instead, pause at different points and ask students to describe what kind of drawing or picture they would create that would fit the text or in some way illustrate what is happening in the story. Encourage students to create brief sketches. (Reassure students that they are expected to make "shorthand" sketches, not polished artwork.)

Once you've read the book and students have completed their sketches, share the book's illustrations with students and guide students to notice the similarities in the important elements that should appear in both the book's illustrations and students' sketches. For example, in Jackie Mims Hopkins' *The Goldminer's Daughter*, Gracie Pearl, in her attempt to get away from evil Mr. Bigglebottom, stomps the Earth so hard that she opens up a natural oil well. At this point in the story, students' sketches might include gushing oil spurting from the Earth because the text implies, and the book's illustrations depict, gushing oil wells.

Distribute copies of Crayon Recaps (pages 73–74). Explain that students will select and read a book of their choosing and use the student pages to complete an illustrated retelling of their story. Provide students with ample time to draw and retell their stories. Allow students to use the art materials or media they prefer. For example, you can have them scan and display their illustrations in a PowerPoint presentation or use clip art to take the place of drawing by hand.

To extend this activity, have students share their stories in small or large groups. Some students may enjoy presenting finished student pages, while others may enjoy narrating and drawing the story at the same time—in much the same way Harold narrates with his purple crayon.

BOOKS FOR MODELING

GRADES 2–4

Thumps, Quack, Moo: A Whacky Adventure by Doreen Cronin (Simon & Schuster, 2008)

Anansi's Party Time by Eric A. Kimmel (Holiday House, 2008)

Louise, the Adventures of a Chicken by Kate DiCamillo (HarperCollins, 2008)

GRADES 4–6

The Goldminer's Daughter: A Melodramatic Fairy Tale by Jackie Mims Hopkins (Peachtree, 2006)

Pssst! by Adam Rex (Harcourt, 2007)

Starlight Goes to Town by Harry Allard (Farrar, Straus and Giroux, 2008)

FICTION BOOKS WORK BEST WITH THIS ACTIVITY.

TECHNOLOGY

TIP ➤ If you are new to digital storytelling, check out these two sites: Interactive Digital Storytelling in Your Classroom at http://its.ksbe.edu/dst and the Center for Digital Storytelling at http://www.storycenter.org.

A student draws and tells the story based on Eric A. Kimmel's *The Greatest of All* (Holiday House, 1991).

Illustrations provide support as the student describes the unfolding storyline.

The completed illustration sequence

Crayon Recaps

When you do a Crayon Recap, you use words and simple line drawings to tell about the characters in your book and what happened to them.

Book title _____

Author _____

On the lines below, tell what your main character(s) looks like. In the box next to the lines, make a drawing of your main character(s).

Main character(s)

_____

_____

_____

On the lines, tell how the story begins. In the box next to the lines, make a drawing of the beginning of your book.

Beginning

_____

_____

Crayon Recaps continued

On the lines, tell about three important events that happened to the character(s). In the boxes next to the lines, make a drawing of each event.

1. _____

_____

_____

_____

2. _____

_____

_____

_____

3. _____

_____

_____

_____

On the lines, tell how the story ends. In the box next to the lines, make a drawing of the ending of your book.

Ending

_____

_____

_____

_____

Points-of-Decision Charts

In every book, characters make decisions that move the story forward to its inevitable conclusion. To better understand the important decisions a character makes and how these decisions affect the story line, students can create a chart like the one included with this activity.

Demonstration & Guided Practice

Select a read-aloud book that features characters whose decisions make a recognizable impact on the story (see suggested titles under Books for Modeling.) Before your read aloud, copy or scan Points-of-Decision Chart (page 76) to display on the board or on screen.

One approach is to read aloud a character-driven picture book, such as John Steptoe's *Mufaro's Beautiful Daughters* (HarperCollins, 1987). After the reading, divide the class into four groups and review the ten-box structure of the chart. On chart paper or on student copies of the reproducible, have two groups create points-of-decision charts for Manyara, the spiteful daughter, and two other groups create charts for Nyasha, the kind daughter. Then let each pair of groups form one group and combine their ideas in a single chart. Display both charts and have volunteers from each group explain how the decisions made by the two daughters involved similar circumstances and people but led to very different outcomes in the end.

Some students may enjoy working with short stories or short graphic novels to follow their characters' decisions. Other students may enjoy taking one event (such as a real-life rescue, battle, or natural disaster) documented in a content-area book and presenting the decisions that were made and the consequences of those decisions.

BOOKS FOR MODELING

GRADES 2–4

Tippy-Tippy-Tippy, Hide! by Candace Fleming (Atheneum Books, 2007)

The Princess Gown by Linda Leopold Strauss (Houghton Mifflin, 2008)

That Book Woman by Heather Henson (Simon & Schuster, 2008)

GRADES 4–6

McFig and McFly: A Tale of Jealousy, Revenge, and Death (With a Happy Ending) by Henrik Drescher (Candlewick, 2008)

Road to Oz by Kathleen Krull (Random House, 2008)

Tire Mountain by Andrea Cheng (Front Street, 2007)

FICTION AND BLENDED BOOKS WORK BEST WITH THIS ACTIVITY.

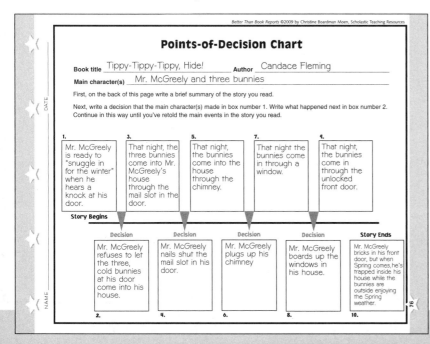

A primary class chart filled in after a second reading of *Tippy-Tippy-Tippy Hide!*

TECHNOLOGY

TIP ➤ Student pairs might present a PowerPoint presentation of the Points-of-Decision Chart. The decision and consequence frames could be set in contrasting colors to demonstrate the decision-consequence relationship.

Points-of-Decision Chart

Book title _____

Main character(s) _____ **Author** _____

First, on the back of this page write a brief summary of the story you read.

Next, write a decision that the main character(s) made in box number 1. Write what happened next in box number 2. Continue in this way until you've retold the main events in the story you read.

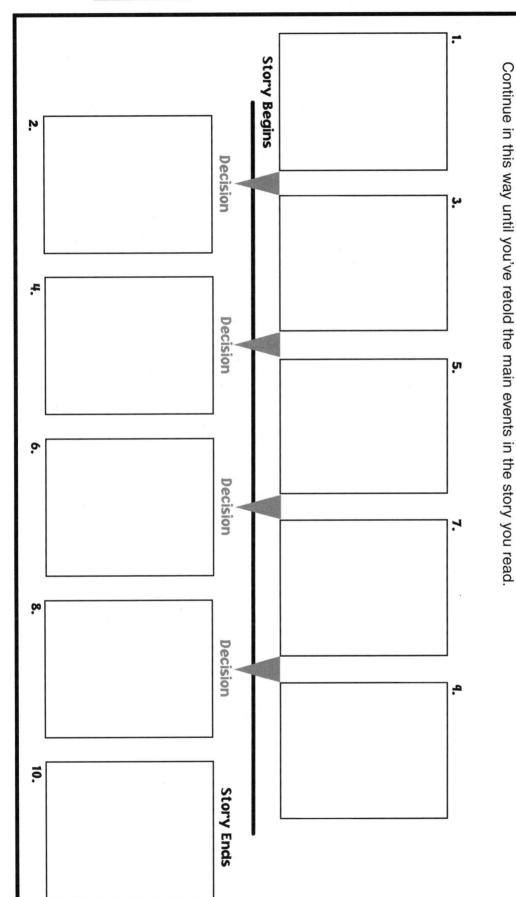

Story Begins

1.

Decision

2.

3.

Decision

4.

5.

Decision

6.

7.

Decision

8.

9.

10.

Story Ends

Grouping Books Together

A text set is a group of related books. The relationship between the different titles is often based on one element. For example, in the text set recommended here for grades 2–4, the common element is the gingerbread character while in the text set for grades 4–6, the common element is heroes of the Holocaust.

The purpose of grouping books is to encourage students to seek out commonalities in a text set while also noting important differences such as topics, themes, character traits, settings, and events.

Demonstration
& Guided Practice

For the purposes of modeling this activity, select a topic that your class has read about and create a graphic organizer based on books you have shared on the topic. Display Grouping Books Together (page 80) on the board or on screen. Eliciting students' input, fill in the titles of books you've read and complete the chart. Alternately, read aloud three books on a shared topic and work collaboratively with students to fill in the chart. (You can look at the samples provided on pages 78 and 79 to guide you. In the first sample, students compare and contrast three fairy tales. In the second example, students compare and contrast a text set of very different books whose common theme is intergenerational relationships.)

Next, divide the class into groups of students and assign or have students select a text set at their independent reading level. (Note: If you do not have multiple copies, groups should read their book together and then rotate books through all of the groups.) If you are using the text set listed for grades 2–4 and want to build background for students who may be unfamiliar with the story, you might first read aloud Paul Galdone's traditional version of the *Gingerbread Boy* (Houghton Mifflin, 1983) or any other traditional version you have available. If you are using the text set for the upper grades, you might first read aloud *A Hero of the Holocaust: The Story of Janusz and His Children* by David A. Adler (Holiday House, 2002).

After reading, ask each group to fill in a copy of the student page, listing the titles of the books across the top of the graphic organizer and the ideas, people, places, or things they're comparing along

BOOKS
FOR
MODELING

GRADES 2–4

Gingerbread Cowboy by Janet Squires (HarperCollins, 2006)

The Gingerbread Girl by Lisa Campbell Ernst (Penguin, 2006)

The Musubi Man: Hawaii's Gingerbread Man by Sandi Takayama (Bess Press, 2007)

GRADES 4–6

Luba: The Angel of Bergen Belsen by Ann Marshal (Tricycle Press, 2003)

Varian Fry: A Hero of the Holocaust by Sean Price (Raintree, 2007)

Passage to Freedom: The Sugihara Story by Ken Mochizuki (Lee & Low, 2003)

FICTION, NONFICTION, AND BLENDED BOOKS WORK BEST WITH THIS ACTIVITY.

TECHNOLOGY

TIP ➤ Invite students to create graphs using the Table feature on Microsoft Windows or XP. Students can create a graphic display and add as many columns (one for each book in their text set) and rows as they wish (one for each attribute they compare).

the side. As a class, discuss the similarities and differences students were able to identify. Invite a volunteer from each group to share other details about his or her group's findings. For example, one group might notice that the books share a common theme (hope), while another group might notice a common element in the setting (a tower).

Finally, invite students to create their own text sets that share a common topic, theme, or plot.

For younger children, you may want to fill in the attributes list in the first column and the book titles at the top of the chart, and then have students complete the chart by writing Xs in the appropriate boxes.

NAME _____ DATE _____

Grouping Books Together

Book sets are books that belong together and are similar in some way. Fill in the chart below to show how the books in your book set are alike and different.

1. Tell what the books in your book set have in common.
   They are fairy tales.

2. Write the titles of the books you read across the top of the chart.

3. Think about how your books have some of the same and some different ideas, people, places, and things. Make a list in the left-hand column.

4. Mark an X in the spaces under each book title if that book has the idea, person, place, or thing named in the left-hand column.

Ideas, people, places, things from the books	Book 1 Beauty and the Beast	Book 2 Snow White	Book 3 Rumpel- stiltskin	Book 4 _____
Evil witch	X	X	X	
Princess		X	Queen	
Prince	X	X	King	
Magic	X	X	X	

Better Than Book Reports ©2009 by Christine Boardman Moen, Scholastic Teaching Resources

80

Distribute a copy of the reproducible to students and explain that each student will read and complete the graphic organizer independently. Some students will be able to identify books that work well together as a text set, while others will need extra support. For younger children, fill in the first column of the chart with the attributes you want students to compare and ask students to write Xs in the appropriate boxes. For older students, suggest that they read books in a series that share the same main character or books written by different authors but share the same setting, such as a specific time period.

This chart illustrates how a group of books shares similar characteristics around the theme of intergenerational friendships.

NAME _____ DATE _____

Grouping Books Together

Book sets are books that belong together and are similar in some way. Fill in the chart below to show how the books in your book set are alike and different.

1. Tell what the books in your book set have in common.
   Friendships between young people and elderly people   .

2. Write the titles of the books you read across the top of the chart.

3. Think about how your books have some of the same and some different ideas, people, places, and things. Make a list in the left-hand column.

4. Mark an X in the spaces under each book title if that book has the idea, person, place, or thing named in the left-hand column.

Ideas, people, places, things from the books	Book 1 The Lemon Sisters	Book 2 What Comes After a Thousand?	Book 3 Granddad's Fishing Buddy	Book 4 Grandfather's Wrinkles
Older and younger character(s) are related			X	X
Younger character learns something new from older character	X	X	X	X
Older character often talks or thinks of past memories	X			X
Story takes place In the country or a rural area		X	X	
Story takes place during the fall		season changes		X
More than one younger character In the story	X			

Better Than Book Reports ©2009 by Christine Boardman Moen, Scholastic Teaching Resources

80

Grouping Books Together

Book sets are books that belong together and are similar in some way. Fill in the chart below to show how the books in your book set are alike and different.

1. Tell what the books in your book set have in common.

_____.

2. Write the titles of the books you read across the top of the chart.

3. Think about how your books have some of the same and some different ideas, people, places, and things. Make a list in the left-hand column.

4. Mark an X in the spaces under each book title if that book has the idea, person, place, or thing named in the left-hand column.

Ideas, people, places, things from the books	Book 1 _____ _____	Book 2 _____ _____	Book 3 _____ _____	Book 4 _____ _____

Better Than Book Reports ©2003 by Christine Boardman Moen, Scholastic Teaching Resources

Sum It Up!

When chapter titles are used in books, their primary function is to express the chapter's main idea. To complete this book-sharing activity, students write chapter titles and brief chapter summaries to support them.

Demonstration & Guided Practice

To introduce students to this activity read aloud "A Lost Button" from Arnold Lobel's *Frog and Toad Are Friends* (HarperCollins, 1979). (Do not tell the students the title of the chapter before you read.) At the end of the reading, ask students to write possible titles for the story as you record them on the board or on screen. Once the group has agreed upon a title, write a brief summary of the chapter.

Select a book to read during your all-class read-aloud time and distribute copies of Sum It Up! (page 82). Explain that after each day's reading, students should write a chapter title and brief summary of the day's reading. Using the activity with your read-aloud ensures that students listen carefully and provide a written demonstration of their listening comprehension. After you have finished reading the book, ask volunteers to share from their collections of chapter titles and summaries. Encourage volunteers to share ways they can apply what they have learned about chapter titles to their everyday reading and content-area reading.

BOOKS FOR MODELING

GRADES 2–4

The Whipping Boy by Sid Fleischman (HarperCollins, 2003, Reprint)

Clever Duck by Dick King-Smith (Roaring Brook Press, 2008)

Oh, Rats! The Story of Rats and People by Albert Marrin (Penguin, 2006)

GRADES 4–6

The Secret of Priest's Grotto by Peter Lane Taylor and Christos Nicola (Kar-Ben, 2007)

Hachiko Waits by Leslea Newsman (Scholastic, 2004)

Ain't Nothing but a Man by Scott Nelson (National Geographic Society, 2007)

FICTION, NONFICTION, AND BLENDED BOOKS WORK BEST WITH THIS ACTIVITY.

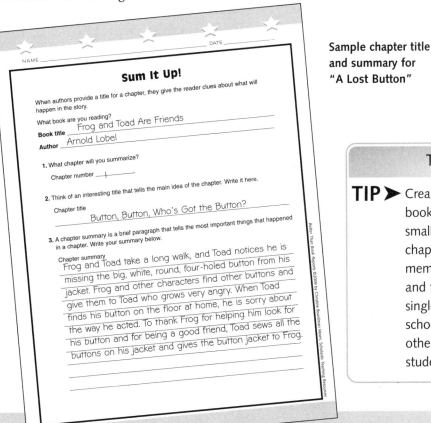

Sample chapter title and summary for "A Lost Button"

TECHNOLOGY

TIP ▶ Create a collaborative summary of the book you read aloud. Divide the class into small groups of students and assign one chapter summary to each group. Group members can synthesize their summaries and then edit, transcribe, and illustrate a single summary. Post the final product on a school-friendly blog or Eboard, where other students and teachers can celebrate student successes.

Sum It Up!

When authors provide a title for a chapter, they give the reader clues about what will happen in the story.

What book are you reading?

Book title _____

Author _____

1. What chapter will you summarize?

   Chapter number _____

2. Think of an interesting title that tells the main idea of the chapter. Write it here.

   Chapter title

   _____

3. A chapter summary is a brief paragraph that tells the most important things that happened in a chapter. Write your summary below.

   Chapter summary

   _____

   _____

   _____

   _____

   _____

   _____

   _____

   _____

   _____

   _____

Fast-Fact Cards

Well-researched, skillfully written nonfiction texts and photo-essay books have become more plentiful and accessible. With this activity, students can share information from these books by focusing on the most interesting or most pertinent facts about everything from athletes to zebras.

Demonstration & Guided Practice

Often informational texts will include additional features such as an index, map, Web sites, and a list of books that can be used for further research. To help students identify and locate important information, invite volunteers to point out these features in the book or books you choose for this activity.

Next, read aloud a portion of the book you've selected. Show students a Fast-Fact Card (page 85) that you've displayed on the board or on screen. As a large group, talk about the format of the card and record the information it should contain. Invite volunteers to make comparisons between the purpose and design of the card they're writing together and other cards with which they are familiar (baseball cards and other trading cards).

Explain that students will be reading books and filling in their own Fast-Fact Cards to gather and share exciting information. Before distributing several copies of the reproducible to each group, invite a volunteer to show how to make the cards—cutting them out, folding them, and attaching the blank sides with tape or glue. (You can determine the number of cards you wish students to create.)

Divide the class into small groups and assign each group a book or a topic for which they can select their own book. After reading, each group should make a list of important details and then decide which facts and statistics they want to use to create a set of Fast-Fact Cards. (Have them write each group member's name on the back of the card at the bottom.)

After all students have created their Fast-Fact Cards, ask groups to exchange sets of cards for reading and comparison. As they share ideas, students can tell which facts they found the most interesting and why. Finally, showcase the card sets to celebrate student work. Place laminated sets in construction paper pockets on a bulletin board or pocket chart. They can also be scanned and displayed on a classroom Web page.

BOOKS FOR MODELING

GRADES 2–4

Nothing but Trouble: The Story of Althea Gibson by Sue Stauffacher (Knopf, 2007)

Sea Horse: The Shyest Fish in the Sea by Chris Butterworth (Candlewick, 2006)

Tracks of a Panda by Nick Downson (Candlewick, 2007)

GRADES 4–6

Sisters & Brothers by Steve Jenkins and Robin Page (Houghton Mifflin, 2008)

Surfer of the Century: The Life of Duke Kahanamoku by Ellie Crowe (Lee & Low, 2007)

We Are the Ship: The Story of Negro League Baseball by Kadir Nelson (Jump at the Sun, 2008)

NONFICTION BOOKS WORK BEST WITH THIS ACTIVITY.

TECHNOLOGY

TIP ➤ Students can use Microsoft Publisher to create nifty-looking Fast-Fact Cards that can be printed in color.

Draw, diagram, or show a photo that tells about your Fast Fact.

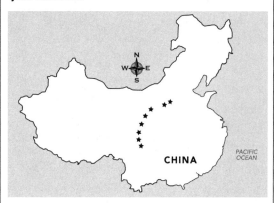

CHINA

PACIFIC OCEAN

It's estimated that only 2,500 wild giant pandas exist today. They mainly live in the high mountain forests in China.

This Fast-Fact Card was created by

Hillary

Fast-Fact Card for *Tracks of a Panda*.
(Back)

Fast-Fact Card

Book title Tracks of a Panda

Author Nick Dowson

Topic Panda Cubs

Fact Panda cubs are very small when they are born. Some are 900 times smaller than their mothers. Panda cubs are also born blind and almost furless. They drink their mother's milk. A panda cub's mother is very protective of her cub.

Fast-Fact Card for *Tracks of a Panda*.
(Front)

Fast-Fact Cards

Fill out the Fast-Fact Card. Then cut along the dotted lines, fold the card in half, and tape or glue the blank sides together.

Fast-Fact Card

Book title _____

Author _____

Topic _____

Fact _____

_____

_____

_____

_____

_____

_____

_____

_____

_____

Draw, diagram, or show a photo that tells about your Fast Fact.

This Fast-Fact Card was created by _____

Plot Predictions

Making predictions about what will happen next is what good readers do to keep themselves actively involved in what they're reading. This critical-thinking skill also helps students increase their comprehension because they reflect on what they're reading and relate it to what they already know. This book-sharing activity will put the action into the transactional art of reading.

Demonstration & Guided Practice

Begin by reading aloud a portion of one of the books listed here. Or if you usually read aloud a longer chapter book to the entire class during your read-aloud time, pause at key points during your read-aloud and ask students to make predictions of what they think will happen next in the story. Also ask students to provide clues or examples from the text to support their predictions about the story's plot.

There are several ways to differentiate this activity. One is to allow students to listen to an audio story or book and pause the audio, make a prediction, and return to the audio to confirm the prediction. To differentiate this activity another way, pause during the read-aloud and have different small groups act out what they think will happen next in the story. A final way to differentiate this activity is to share a graphic novel with students, pause while sharing the book, and ask students to draw what they think should be the next scene in the book.

Once students have participated in the demonstration of this activity, and you've guided them through the process of making predictions supported by information from the text (or inferential information), ask students to select a book to read. Distribute copies of Plot Predictions (page 88) and explain that each student will read a portion of the book he or she selected and then record predictions about what will happen next in the story. To encourage students to make several predictions in one sitting, you may want to have students use sticky notes of different colors that they can place in their books as they read (assign one color for predictions, another color for reasons to support the predictions, and a third color for the actual outcome). Sticky notes can be labeled with quick notes or reminders (e.g., "Prediction 1: no escape from cave") and then organized on a sheet of paper to show students' line of thinking and the outcome for each prediction.

BOOKS FOR MODELING

GRADES 2–4

Goldie Socks and the Three Libearians by Jackie Mims Hopkins (Upstart Books, 2007)

The Perfect Nest by Catherine Friend (Candlewick, 2007)

Too Many Toys by David Shannon (Blue Sky Press, 2008)

GRADES 4–6

A Taste of Colored Water by Matt Faulkner (Simon & Schuster, 2008)

The Lemonade Club by Patricia Polacco (Philomel, 2007)

Zen Ties by Jon J. Muth (Scholastic, 2008)

FICTION BOOKS WORK BEST WITH THIS ACTIVITY.

TECHNOLOGY

TIP ➤ The easiest way for students to practice making predictions is to listen to an audio book. These are readily available from most public libraries. Explain that students should stop the CD or audiotape from time to time and then use their student page to record what they think might happen next in the story. For older students, this is an especially purposeful activity when they listen to mystery stories.

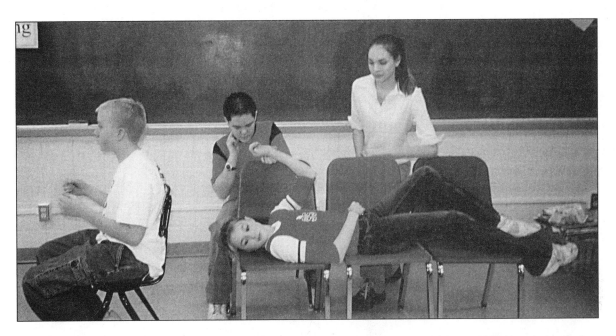

This group of students acts out a scene they predict will happen next during a pause in a teacher read-aloud of a short story. The group predicts that the main character will be involved in a traffic accident and be taken to a hospital in an ambulance.

During a teacher read-aloud or a student paired-reading, you may want students to draw what they think will happen next in the story.

In *14 Cows for America* by Carmen Agra Deedy (Peachtree, 2009) Kimeli, who has been studying in America to become a doctor, returns to his village in Kenya and tells the people there of the attack of September 11, 2001. Before they read about Kimeli's return, students draw what they think will be the reactions of the Maasai who ". . . are fierce when provoked, but easily moved to kindness when they hear of suffering or injustice."

Plot Predictions

Read a part of your book and think about what you've read. Make some guesses, or predictions, about what you think will happen next in the story.

Book title _____

Author _____

Think About

- what has happened in your story so far

- the book's characters and what they're like

- where the story is taking place

- how the story makes you feel

Think About

- what you already know about the beginnings, middles, and endings of stories

- what you already know about characters and how they act

- what you already know about the story's setting

Tell what you think will happen next in the story.

_____

_____

_____

_____

Explain why you think this will happen. Tell several reasons for your prediction. If you need more room, write on the back of this page.

_____

_____

_____

_____

Cornering the Conflict

Because it's sometimes difficult for students to understand the literary element of conflict, it might be helpful for them to think of conflict as the main struggle that takes place in the story. Using the student page for support, students can ask themselves a series of questions to help determine a story's main conflict.

Demonstration & Guided Practice

To begin, read aloud one of the stories listed here or another book that complements your curriculum. Copy on the board the questions and chart from Cornering the Conflict (pages 91 and 92) or display them on screen. Work as a group to identify the main conflict in the book you read aloud and complete the activity. Although you may not want to teach the formal names for the four types of conflict, be sure to give examples of each: person versus person, person versus nature, person versus society, and person versus him- or herself.

Divide the class into small groups of students. Distribute a copy of the two student pages to each group. Explain that students should work collaboratively to select a book to read and then complete the pages once all group members have read the book. When groups have finished the assignment, have students compare and contrast the different types of conflict represented in their books.

Once students have participated in this group activity, ask them to read a book on a topic of their choosing and complete the Cornering the Conflict student pages to tell about the conflicts in the book.

BOOKS FOR MODELING

GRADES 2–4

Fletcher and the Falling Leaves by Julia Rawlington (HarperCollins, 2008, Reprint)

Benny and Penny in Just Pretend by Geoffrey Hayes (Raw Junior, 2008)

Dimity Dumpty: The Story of Humpty's Little Sister by Bob Graham (Candlewick, 2007)

GRADES 4–6

Seeing the Elephant: A Story of the Civil War by Pat Hughes (Farrar, Straus and Giroux, 2007)

Walking to School by Eve Bunting (Houghton Mifflin, 2008)

Finding Home by Sandra Markle (Charlesbridge, 2008)

FICTION AND BLENDED BOOKS WORK BEST WITH THIS ACTIVITY.

TECHNOLOGY

TIP ➤ Have students use a Microsoft Publisher program or Inspiration program to design their own graphic organizers. Organizers are also easy to create using the tool bar of your interactive whiteboard program.

NAME _____ DATE _____

Cornering the Conflict

Think about the main character in the book you read and the most important conflict or struggle he or she faced. Answer the questions below.

Book title _Mice Twice_

Author _Joseph Law_

1. Does the main character struggle with another character? If so, give an example.
Mouse struggles with Cat, who wants to eat him.
_____

2. Does the main character struggle with storms, hurricanes, forest fires, or any other acts of nature? If so, give an example.
No. Mouse tries not to get eaten by Cat.
_____

3. Does the main character struggle with being afraid, lonely, unhappy, or angry? If so, give an example.
No. Cat and Mouse were angry at each other.
_____

4. Does the main character struggle with rules, laws, or customs that he or she is expected to obey? If so, give an example.
_No._
_____

For example, after reading Joseph Low's Caldecott Honor Book *Mice Twice* (Simon & Schuster, 2005 RP), a completed conflict organizer might be similar to the one at left.

If you choose to use *Mice Twice* during your Demonstration and Guided Practice session, you and your students can use this sheet to fill in the diagram and complete the sentence, which helps identify the story's main conflict.

NAME _____ DATE _____

Cornering the Conflict continued

Check the statements that are true. Follow the directions to complete the chart below.

☐ The main character struggled with other characters. (Write the names of these characters in corner #1.)

☐ The main character struggled with storms, fires, or other natural disasters. (Write the natural disaster in corner #2.)

☐ The main character struggled with his or her fears, loneliness, unhappiness, or anger. (Write the emotion or feeling in corner #3.)

☐ The main character struggled with rules, laws, or customs that she or he was supposed to obey. (Write the rule, law, or custom in corner #4.)

1 — Cat

Mouse
Name of main character
AGAINST

4

2

3

Describe the main conflict in one or two sentences.
The main conflict was Mouse tried not to get eaten by Cat.
_____
_____

Cornering the Conflict

Think about the main character in the book you read and the most important conflict or struggle he or she faced. Answer the questions below.

Book title _____

Author _____

1. Does the main character struggle with another character? If so, give an example.

_____

_____

2. Does the main character struggle with storms, hurricanes, forest fires, or any other acts of nature? If so, give an example.

_____

_____

3. Does the main character struggle with being afraid, lonely, unhappy, or angry? If so, give an example.

_____

_____

4. Does the main character struggle with rules, laws, or customs that he or she is expected to obey? If so, give an example.

_____

_____

Cornering the Conflict continued

Check the statements that are true. Follow the directions to complete the chart below.

☐ The main character struggled with other characters.
(Write the names of these characters in corner #1.)

☐ The main character struggled with storms, fires, or other
natural disasters. (Write the natural disaster in corner #2.)

☐ The main character struggled with his or her fears, loneliness,
unhappiness, or anger. (Write the emotion or feeling in corner #3.)

☐ The main character struggled with rules, laws, or customs that she
or he was supposed to obey. (Write the rule, law, or custom in corner #4.)

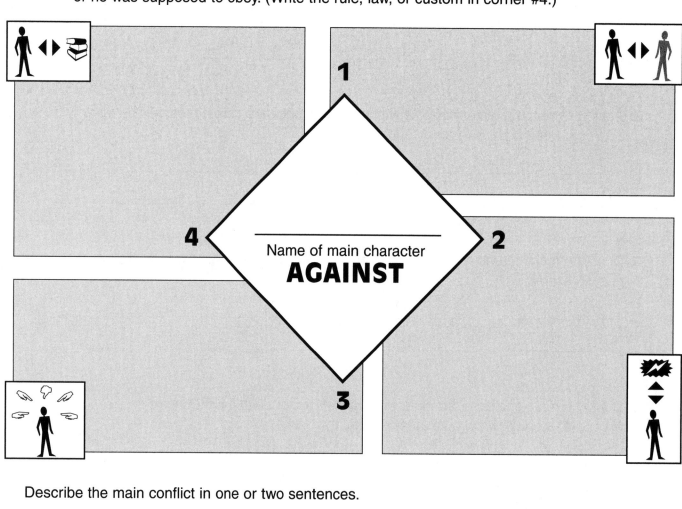

1

4

2

_____
Name of main character
AGAINST

3

Describe the main conflict in one or two sentences.

_____

_____

_____

_____

Tell-Along Boards

A Tell-Along Board is a creative book-sharing activity that combines storytelling, puppetry, and art. Students create small, hand-held puppets of the main characters. They also illustrate scenes from the book on poster board. Finally, students cut a lengthwise slit in the poster board so the puppets can be moved from setting to setting during the storytelling.

Demonstration
& Guided Practice

Before you introduce this activity, read a story and then create your own puppets and three-scene Tell-Along Board to share with the class. When your models are complete, retell the story aloud. As you speak, manipulate the puppet through the scenes on the Tell-Along Board. As a group, talk about what steps you had to take, from selecting a book to read to making the board and puppets. Reinforce the idea that you had to plan, prepare, and practice in order to be successful.

Next, divide the class into small groups and ask each group to choose a book to read and retell. Distribute copies of Tell-Along Boards: Planning Checklist (page 94). Explain that students should use their planning pages to help them plan and construct their Tell-Along Boards, which they will use as props for a short retelling of the book they've read and to demonstrate what they understand about their book's characters, setting, beginning, middle, and end.

BOOKS FOR MODELING

GRADES 2–4

Big Chickens Fly the Coop by Leslie Helakoski (Penguin, 2008)

Duck at the Door by Jackie Urbanovic (HarperCollins, 2007)

Millie Waits for the Mail by Alexander Steffensmeier (Walker & Co., 2007)

GRADES 4–6

Ms. McCaw Learns to Draw by Kaethe Zemach (Arthur Levine, 2008)

Louise, The Adventures of a Chicken by Kate DiCamillo (Joanna Cotler Books, 2008)

The Birthday Tree by Paul Fleischman (Candlewick, 2008)

FICTION BOOKS WORK BEST WITH THIS ACTIVITY.

In this multi-scene board describing Louis Sachar's *Holes*, a student uses several manipulative pieces, including a pair of falling sneakers, to dramatize the action.

T E C H N O L O G Y

TIP ➤ Encourage students to add music or sound effects to their retellings. Sound effects CDs and music CDs are readily available in many public libraries and through interlibrary loan programs, and may also be downloaded from the Web. (Search for "free sound effects" on your browser.)

TELL-ALONG BOARDS

Planning Checklist

Follow the directions on this page to plan for your story retelling.

Tell about the book you read.

Book title _____

Author _____

Illustrator _____

The main character is _____

After you complete each task below, place a check mark in the box.

☐ **1.** On the back of this page, write the important events in the story in the order they happened.

☐ **2.** Write where each event took place. Be sure to include where the main character is at the beginning and ending of the story.

☐ **3.** Circle the three most important, or memorable, events. Later you will use your puppet and Tell-Along Board to retell these events.

☐ **4.** To make your puppet and Tell-Along Board, you will likely need heavy paper or poster board, craft sticks, scissors, glue, pencils, and markers. List any additional materials you will need here:

_____.

☐ **5.** Draw the main character on heavy paper. Color it, cut it out, and tape it to a craft stick to create a stick puppet. If another character should be included in the retelling, make a puppet of that character as well.

☐ **6.** Divide a large piece of heavy paper or poster board into three sections. In each section, draw the scene where an important event happened (the setting).

☐ **7.** Draw a line on the poster board to show where the puppet will travel through the scenes. Cut along this line so the puppet can stick through and move from setting to setting.

☐ **8.** Practice moving the hand puppet through the different scenes while retelling the story.

☐ **9.** Retell the story you read to the class using the puppet and Tell-Along Board you created.

Changing the World: Biographies

Inventors, world leaders, and ordinary people are among the many who have changed the world in ways both big and small. By reading biographies, students may come to realize that they, too, have the opportunity to impact the world in positive ways.

Demonstration & Guided Practice

To introduce this activity, invite volunteers to name some people who have changed the world for the better. Explain that a biography is a book written about a person's life. That person may have been famous. Or, that person may have led an ordinary life.

Read aloud one of the books listed here or another book that complements your curriculum. Invite a volunteer to draw a picture of the person you read about, including details from the book (maybe a peaked hat, horn-rimmed glasses, or curly wig). Then, as a group, answer the questions from Changing the World: Biographies (page 97). Discuss the ways in which the person you read about addressed challenges and affected change.

Once students have demonstrated their understanding of the activity, explain that they should select a biography to read. Distribute copies of the reproducible and ask students to complete it by working independently, with a partner, or in small groups.

BOOKS FOR MODELING

GRADES 2–4

John Muir: America's First Environmentalist by Kathryn Lasky (Candlewick, 2008)

Boys of Steel: The Creators of Superman by Marc Tyler Nobleman (Knopf, 2008)

Wangari's Trees of Peace: A True Story From Africa by Jeannette Winter (Harcourt, 2008)

GRADES 4–6

Planting the Trees of Kenya: The Story of Wangari Maathai by Claire A. Nivola (Farrar, Straus and Giroux, 2008)

Down the Colorado: John Wesley Powell, the One-Armed Explorer by Deborah Kogan Ray (Farrar, Straus and Giroux, 2007)

Road to Oz by Kathleen Krull (Random House, 2008)

BIOGRAPHY AND BLENDED BOOKS WORK BEST WITH THIS ACTIVITY.

EDGAR ALLAN POE: NOVELIST, POET, AND CREATOR OF THE DETECTIVE STORY

Book Title: *Nevermore: A Photobiography of Edgar Allan Poe* Author: Karen E. Lanage

1. **What did the person learn, practice or enjoy doing as she or he was growing up?**
Poe, whose mother died at age 24 and whose father abandoned him, was raised by Frances and John Allan and lived in Richmond, Virginia, for much of his early life. He received a "gentleman's education." He attended a boarding school in London when he was younger and the University of Virginia and the United States Military Academy at West Point when he was older. He enjoyed writing poetry and reading.

2. **What failures or struggles did this person have before he or she was successful?**
Poe did not get paid much for his writing because there were no copyright laws at the time. He often did not have enough money to live on. After his wife died, he lost many jobs and also drank a lot.

3. **What was this person's main accomplishment?**
Poe created the detective story. Baltimore's National Football League team is named after his most famous poem, "The Raven." Poe's writing also influenced other early American writers.

4. **What does this person's accomplishment mean to you? How has it affected your life?**
I enjoy mystery stories and horror movies. I think without Edgar Allan Poe, these kinds of stories and movies would not be as interesting.

5. **How has this person's accomplishment affected the world?**
Poe influenced Sir Arthur Conan Doyle who wrote the Sherlock Holmes detective stories. Poe also wrote stories and poetry that are still read and appreciated 200 years after his death.

Guided by five questions from Changing the World: Biographies (page 97), a student creates a short, but informative biography of poet Edgar Allan Poe.

TECHNOLOGY

TIP ➤ Authors often use primary sources when researching to gather information for a biography. To help students to begin to learn about primary sources and how to use them, visit the Library of Congress' Web site at http://lcweb2.loc.gov. It has a special section titled Using Primary Sources in the Classroom. Students can also use this resource to locate historical documents, photographs, and maps.

CHANGING THE WORLD

Biographies

Read a biography of a person whose life interests you. Use the information you gather to complete these pages.

Book title _____

Author _____

HINT

As you read, you might want to keep a note card in your book so you can write down page numbers, names, and events that will help you answer the questions on page 97.

In the picture frame, draw a picture of the person you read about. Include details from the book (such as a distinctive hat, glasses, or piece of clothing).

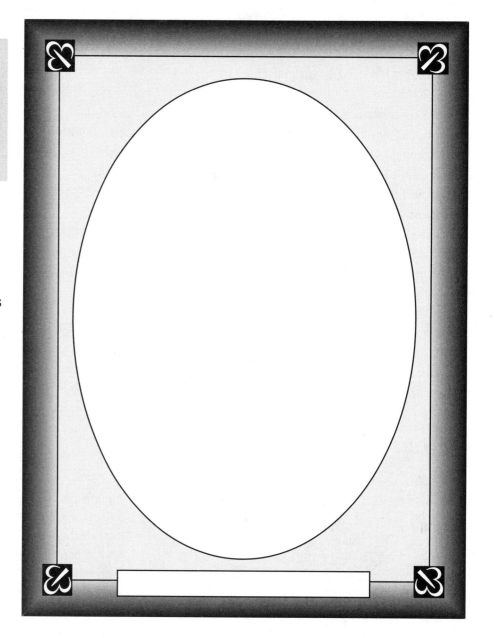

CHANGING THE WORLD

Biographies

1. What did the person learn, practice, or enjoy doing as she or he was growing up?

_____

_____

_____

2. What failures or struggles did this person have before he or she was successful?

_____

_____

_____

3. What was this person's main accomplishment?

_____

_____

_____

4. What does this person's accomplishment mean to you? How has it affected your life?

_____

_____

_____

5. How has this person's accomplishment affected the world?

_____

_____

_____

PERSONification Webs

Although students may not be familiar with the term, they probably are familiar with personification, a literary device in which inanimate objects or abstractions possess human qualities. Any student who has seen a cartoon car talk, a tree whistle, or a pair of shoes dance and sing knows about personification and working on this book-sharing activity will buttress that knowledge.

Demonstration & Guided Practice

As a group, begin this activity by discussing how robot, car, and toy cartoon characters are personified. Have students gather into small groups, with one group responsible for making a list of robot characters that share feelings while another group makes a list of machines that talk (Jon Scieszka's *Trucktown* Series [Simon & Schuster, 2008] is one resource). You might have another group make a list of toys that come alive and so on. Have a volunteer from each group share their list of characters with the rest of the class.

Read aloud one of the books from the suggested list such as *Rosebud and Red Flannel*. Distribute copies of Personification Webs (page 99) and guide students as they complete the web organizer.

When students are ready, have them choose an independent reading book in which the main character is a nonhuman object that takes on human characteristics.

BOOKS FOR MODELING

GRADES 2–4

Toy Boat by Randall de Seve (Penguin, 2007)

Smitten by David Gordon (Simon & Schuster, 2007)

Timothy and the Strong Pajamas by Viviane Schwarz (Arthur Levine, 2007)

GRADES 4–6

The Pencil by Allan Ahlzberg (Candlewick Press, 2008)

Rosebud and Red Flannel by Ethel Pochocki (Down East Books, 2003)

Darkness Slipped In by Ella Burfoot (Roaring Book Press, 2008)

FICTION BOOKS WORK BEST WITH THIS ACTIVITY.

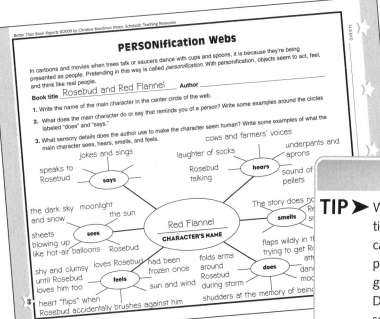

A sample PERSONification Web for *Rosebud and Red Flannel*

TECHNOLOGY

TIP ➤ With advances in technology, showing personification in film has moved from cartoons to sophisticated animation. Consider showing students brief portions of animated cartoons or movies that are good examples of personification. Many Disney and Disney Pixar movies, such as *Toy Story*, contain personification and contain age-appropriate content.

PERSONiFication Webs

In cartoons and movies when trees talk or saucers dance with cups and spoons, it is because they're being presented as people. Pretending in this way is called *personification*. With personification, objects seem to act, feel, and think like real people.

Book title _____

Author _____

1. Write the name of the main character in the center circle of the web.

2. What does the main character do or say that reminds you of a person? Write some examples around the circles labeled "does" and "says."

3. What sensory details does the author use to make the character seem human? Write some examples of what the main character sees, hears, smells, and feels.

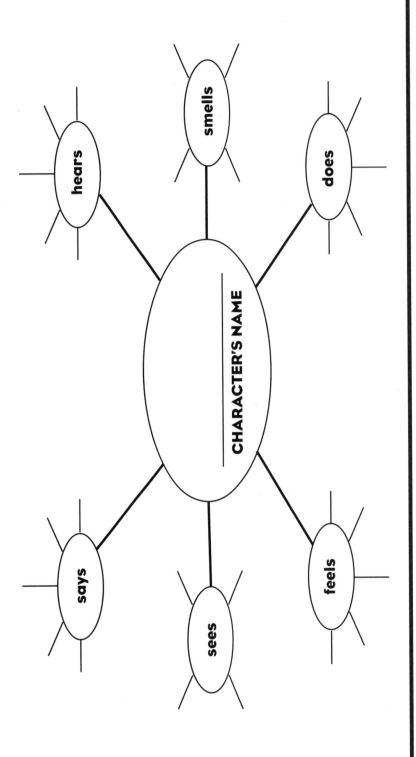

Opinion Pages

When a small group of students read the same book, not all members of the group may enjoy the same scenes or feel the same about different characters. This activity will help students understand that one book may not please every reader because, like books, every reader is unique. Students also learn that every reader is entitled to his or her own opinion.

Demonstration & Guided Practice

Distribute copies of Opinion Page (page 102) and, as a group, discuss the ways in which individual tastes and background experiences affect our opinions. Divide the class into several small groups. Give each trio of students a copy of one of the books listed here or other books that align with your curriculum.

Explain that each group of students will read the same story or story passages. However, each child should complete his or her own student page. Once members of each group have recorded their personal opinions, members should compare and contrast the differences among their perspectives.

When all groups have finished, ask a volunteer from each group to report their findings to the class or take turns reporting to the other small groups. Here is one way to engage three members from each small group:

- One group member holds up a copy of the book and briefly retells the story.

- One group member tells how the group's opinions were alike.

- One group member tells how the group's opinions were different.

A different approach to investigating how opinions develop involves allowing different small groups of students to select different brief chapters or sections from *First Kids: The True Stories of All the Presidents' Children*. With dozens of stories from which to choose, students will find learning about the lives of the many children who spent time living in the White House engaging and enlightening. When their reading is done, have student groups move about the room as they share brief summaries and opinions about what they've read. When students are ready, they should select a book to read independently and record their insights and opinions on a copy of page 102.

BOOKS FOR MODELING

GRADES 2–4

The Black Book of Colors by Menena Cottin (Groundwood Books, 2008)

A Home for Dixie: The True Story of a Rescued Puppy by Emma Jackson (HarperCollins, 2008)

Our Friendship Rules by Peggy Moss (Tilbury House, 2007)

GRADES 4–6

Angel Girl by Laurie Friedman (Lerner, 2008)

One Hen: How One Small Loan Made a Big Difference by Katie Smith Milway (Kids Can Press, 2008)

First Kids: The True Stories of All the Presidents' Children by Noah McCullough (Scholastic, 2008)

FICTION, NONFICTION, AND BLENDED BOOKS WORK BEST WITH THIS ACTIVITY.

A trio of students read book reviews from various Web sites about a book they've read and loved. They discuss whether they agree or disagree with the reviews. This trio decided that the reviews from three different Web sites, which were all positive, validated their opinions of the book.

TECHNOLOGY

TIP ➤ Encourage students to read other people's opinions on the Web regarding books, movies, or any topic about which students are interested. Monitor their research as they read reviews and opinion polls on age-appropriate magazines and news sources.

Opinion Page

Use the sentence frames below to tell your opinion (what you think) about the book you've read. Include reference details such as page and paragraph numbers.

Book title _____

Author _____

1. My favorite part of the story was _____

_____

_____

page(s) _____   paragraph(s) _____

2. I liked the story when the character said _____

_____

_____

page(s) _____   paragraph(s) _____

3. I felt (circle one)   **happy   sad   scared   excited   surprised   bored**

(add your own) _____   when _____

_____

_____

page(s) _____   paragraph(s) _____

4. The story's (circle one)   **plot   character(s)   setting**

reminded me of _____

_____

_____

page(s) _____   paragraph(s) _____

Better Than Book Reports ©2009 by Christine Boardman Moen, Scholastic Teaching Resources

Notable Quotables

Students familiar with famous quotations have background knowledge they will draw upon as they progress through school. Knowing the time, place, and circumstances of resonant quotes in literature and in history is knowledge that can scaffold future learning. In this book-sharing activity students explore the significance of quotes said during historically significant times or during events that impacted a particular story character deeply.

Demonstration & Guided Practice

Introduce students to the idea of quotes by playing a simple game that invites students to recall familiar quotes and storybook passages. To begin, tell students you are going to read some famous quotations and they are to identify who said the words in the quotation. (You can display choices of names from which students can choose.) Use quotations such as "I have a dream . . ." from *Martin's Big Words* by Doreen Rappaport (Hyperion, 2007) to "I'll huff and I'll puff, and I'll blow your house down" from the story of "The Three Little Pigs" to Neil Armstrong's words as he first walked on the moon in 1969: "That's one small step for man; one giant leap for mankind."

If you have a class set of whiteboards, students can record and show their answers, providing you with quick access to their understanding. Older students can write their answers on sticky notes and put their notes under the name of their choice from the names on display. After students respond with their choices, as a group discuss why some quotes and story passages remain memorable. Discuss the role of historical context and the lasting appeal of tales like "The Three Little Pigs."

Select a book to read aloud to the group. As you read, pause from time to time to ask students if they have heard a person or character say something notable, a phrase or sentiment that seems to hold special meaning. Invite several volunteers to explain why particular excerpts may be significant. When the group is ready, distribute copies of Notable Quotables (page 105). Explain that students will select a book and read independently, then use the student page to record significant or memorable lines from the story.

BOOKS FOR MODELING

GRADES 2–4

Winston of Churchill by Jean Davies Okimoto (Sasquatch Books, 2007)

We the People: The Story of Our Constitution by Lynne Cheney (Simon & Schuster, 2008)

Lincoln and Douglass: An American Friendship by Nikki Giovanni ((Holt, 2008)

GRADES 4–6

Farmer George Plants a Nation by Peggy Thomas (Calkins Creek, 2008)

Team Moon: How 400,000 People Landed Apollo 11 on the Moon by Catherine Thimmesh (Houghton Mifflin, 2006)

Our White House: Looking in, Looking Out by The National Children's Book and Literacy Alliance (Candlewick Press, 2008)

FICTION, NONFICTION, AND BLENDED BOOKS WORK BEST WITH THIS ACTIVITY.

TECHNOLOGY

TIP ➤ Students may enjoy exploring famous quotes at http://www.quotationspage.com, which allows students to search by author and subject. Students can also search the Columbia Encyclopedia at http://www.bartleby.com.100/.

Excerpted from fiction or nonfiction books, these selected quotations help students focus on key ideas or themes.

Book title The Life & Art of Wayne Thiebaud: Delicious

Author Susan Goldman Rubin

Quote " I tried to steal every kind of idea—Western, Eastern —and the use of everything I could think of, size differences, color differences . . . exaggeration. "

Quote said by Wayne Thiebaud   page(s) 73

It is important in the story because it tells that Wayne Thiebaud always worked to make his paintings better, so he tried different styles.

Book title Washington at Valley Forge

Author Russell Freedman

Quote " Colonel Cobb, if you are afraid, you have the liberty to step back. "

Quote said by George Washington   page(s) 75

It is important in the story because it shows how brave Washington was. Washington always put himself in the middle of the fighting, and at the

Battle of Yorktown, he told his aide he could go for cover, but he (Washington) wasn't going to.

Book title The Anne Frank Case: Simon Wiesenthal's Search for the Truth

Author Susan Goldman Rubin

Quote " I had no one anymore. No family, no friends. Someone had to live on and tell what it was really like. "

Quote said by Simon Wiesenthal   page(s) 73

It is important in the story because this is when Simon decides to help the Americans search for war criminals, which became a life-long goal of his.

Notable Quotables

Story characters and famous people are often remembered for their words. These words may be especially notable because they were said during historically significant times or during events that affected the character or person deeply.

Get started creating your own collection of memorable lines by recording quotes from the book you've just read. Be sure to record the words exactly and then describe why the quote is important to the story.

Book title _____

Author _____

Quote " _____

_____

_____ "

Quote said by _____ page(s) _____

It is important in the story because _____

_____

Book title _____

Author _____

Quote " _____

_____

_____ "

Quote said by _____ page(s) _____

It is important in the story because _____

_____

Synonym Strips

Designed to help students broaden their vocabularies, this activity challenges students to generate lists of synonyms. Students then use the synonyms as anchors, tethering unfamiliar words to familiar ones.

Demonstration & Guided Practice

Read aloud one of the books listed here or one that aligns with your curriculum. Explain that as you read a brief passage the group should listen for unfamiliar words. (Note: Having students use a "thumbs up" sign when they hear an unfamiliar word is an easy way to assess students' word knowledge.) You may need to record the words for younger students, while older students may make individual word lists. Encourage students to use context clues to help them understand the unfamiliar words they encounter.

From students' lists, select one word to use for modeling the synonym activity. On a sentence strip, copy the sentence in which the word appears in the text. Underline the unfamiliar word. Next, guide students as they analyze the sentence to determine the word's function within the sentence. (Does the word describe, name, show action, etc.?) Next, read the sentence aloud and ask volunteers to suggest synonyms for the unfamiliar word. If students are unable to provide synonyms, encourage them to use a thesaurus. The synonyms should be familiar so that students can anchor the new vocabulary word to these known words and weave the new word into their working knowledge.

Once students have provided you with two or three synonyms, have the entire group read aloud the sentence inserting the synonym directly after reading the vocabulary word. For example, the unfamiliar word in this sentence from *The Greatest Story Never Told* is *commotion*. "Late that evening, Nurse Linda heard a loud commotion coming from room 714." Students would read aloud the following: Late that evening, Nurse Linda heard a loud commotion—*disturbance*—coming from room 714."

To differentiate this activity, divide the class into groups and give each group a copy of the same book. Group members should read a passage from the book together and develop a list of unfamiliar words, with each student supplying one word. The groups then copy the sentences that provide context onto sentence strips and work together to recall or look up appropriate synonyms to record on the backside of each strip. After the groups are done with their work, a volunteer from each

BOOKS FOR MODELING

GRADES 2–4

Coral Reefs by Gail Gibbons (Holiday House, 2007)

Tupelo Rides the Rails by Melissa Sweet (Houghton Mifflin, 2008)

Two Bobbies: A True Story of Hurricane Katrina, Friendship, and Survival by Kirby Larson (Walker & Co., 2008)

GRADES 4–6

Lady Liberty: A Biography by Doreen Rappaport (Candlewick, 2008)

Johnny Appleseed by Jane Yolen (HarperCollins, 2008)

The Greatest Story Never Told by Ray Negron (HarperCollins, 2008)

FICTION, NONFICTION, AND BLENDED BOOKS WORK BEST WITH THIS ACTIVITY.

TECHNOLOGY

TIP ➤ The Merriam Webster's online thesaurus can be found at http://www.merriam-webster.com. It's easy for students to use and also allows students to search for synonyms in languages other than English.

group reads aloud his or her group's collection of unfamiliar words in combination with the sentence strips and synonyms.

Book title Tupelo Rides the Rails   **Author** Melissa Sweet

Sentence 1: Later, Garbage Pail Tex regaled them with tales of dog heroes: of Toto's adventures with Dorothy, of Krypto, Superman's valiant dog, and of Lassie and her boy Timmy.   (page _____)

entertained   delighted   amused

Book title Fire and Silk: Flying in a Hot Air Balloon   **Author** Neil Johnson

---

Sentence 1: It's fun to look out from an airborne balloon and see other colorful and majestic balloons flying nearby.   (page 25)

splendid   grand   impressive

Book title Charlotte's Web   **Author** E. B. White

Sentence 1: Mr. Zuckerman heard, and he came out of the machine shed where he was mending a tool.   (page 18)

fixing   repairing

Synonym Strips

One way to become a better reader is to increase your vocabulary by learning synonyms for unfamiliar words. A synonym is a word whose meaning is similar to another word. For example, *clock* is a synonym for *chronometer*.

1. Record the book title and author.
2. Cut the strips along the dotted lines. Fold them back along the solid fold lines.
3. From your reading, find four words that are unfamiliar to you and bookmark them.
4. On a strip, copy the sentence where you found the unfamiliar word, underline the word, and note the page number.
5. Using a thesaurus, select two synonyms that match the meaning of the word as it is used in the book. Record the synonyms on the back of the strip.
6. Read the sentence on the front of the strip. Replace the underlined word with a synonym. Then repeat this process with the other synonym.

Book title _____ Author _____

Sentence 1: _____ (page _____)

Sentence 2: _____ (page _____)

Sentence 3: _____ (page _____)

Sentence 4: _____ (page _____)

Better Than Book Reports ©2003 by Christine Boardman Moen, Scholastic Teaching Resources

Thank You Notes

Writing an e-mail thank you note for a small kindness is certainly appropriate, but many people still enjoy receiving thank you notes that arrive in the mail and acknowledge acts of generosity and thoughtfulness. In fact, many people consider the etiquette of writing thank you notes a life-long literacy skill.

Demonstration
& Guided Practice

For each grade group in Books for Modeling, you'll find a suggested book written specifically to teach students how to compose thank you notes. The other suggested books are stories in which characters write or receive thank you notes. The hilarious *Thank You, Aunt Tallulah* is recommended for both age groups of students.

As a group, make a list of the acts of kindnesses for which students are thankful. You can also make a list of people for whom students' are grateful. Explain that students will be writing real thank you notes that they will mail. They will write for the authentic purpose of saying "Thank you" to a person for a particular act or perpetual thoughtfulness.

Provide students with a copy of Thank You Notes (page 110). Discuss the information that should be contained in the body of the note, and point out the parts of the note students should include, such as the date, greeting, and salutation. Then have students compose their notes, follow directions to fold the notes into a self-contained envelope, add the addresses on the outside, and stick on a stamp. Finally, mail them!

April 7, 2009

Dear Billy,

Thank you for always being there for me. I would also like to thank you for going into the airforce and serving our country. I love you very much and miss you, too!

Sincerely,
Amy
P.S. Miss you very much!

April 7, 2009

Dear Dad,

Thank you for your help with my science fair project. Without you I would have never made it as far as I did. So for all of your support and patience with me, thank you.

With great love,
John
P.S.

BOOKS FOR MODELING

GRADES 2–4

The Kids' Guide to Writing Great Thank-You Notes by Jean Summers (Writers' Collective, 2005)

Thank You, Aunt Tallulah by Carmela Lavigna Coyle (Rising Moon, 2006)

Do Unto Otters: A Book About Manners by Laurie Keller (Henry Holt, 2007)

GRADES 4–6

One Thousand Tracings by Lita Judge (Hyperion Books, 2007)

Thank You, Aunt Talulah by Carmela Lavigna Coyle (Rising Moon, 2006)

The Art of Thank You: Crafting Notes of Gratitude by Connie Leas (Atria Books, 2002)

FICTION, NONFICTION, AND BLENDED BOOKS WORK BEST WITH THIS ACTIVITY.

TECHNOLOGY

TIP ➤ Many students may be unfamiliar with writing and receiving letters. Consider taking this activity further by inviting students to research past and present services provided by the United States Postal Service at http://www.usps.com/postalhistory.

Thank You Notes

1. Write a thank you note.
   Proofread what you have written.
2. Cut along the edges.
3. Fold the flaps into the center. Tape to close.
4. Turn the thank you note over and address the outside of the envelope. Add a stamp where it belongs.
5. Mail it.

Body

Date

Closing

Signature

Postscript

Salutation

P. S.

Cause-and-Effect Organizers

Understanding the links between causes and effects can sometimes be challenging for students. With this book-sharing activity students gain practice using a graphic organizer especially designed to help them "see" the cause-effect relationships more readily and strengthen developing comprehension skills.

Demonstration
& Guided Practice

Begin this book-sharing activity with a simple demonstration of the cause-effect relationship. For example, you might turn off the classroom's lights for a moment and then as a group discuss briefly the effects of your action.

When the group demonstrates understanding of the cause-effect relationship, read about the destruction of rain forests or another high-interest nonfiction topic. You might share a brief article, a section from a content-area textbook, or a picture book on the topic. Invite students to identify causes and effects of the problem. Divide the class into small groups of students. Provide each group with a copy of Cause-and-Effect Organizers: Multiple Effects (page 113), and ask a volunteer from each group to record the group's responses.

Next, provide each group of students with a copy of Cause-and-Effect Organizers: Multiple Causes (page 114). Point out that the first graphic organizer showed one cause producing multiple effects. The second organizer invites students to think about multiple causes producing one significant effect. Explain that after the groups have completed both graphic organizers, each student is responsible for selecting a book and completing one (or both!) of the graphic organizers independently.

Content-area textbooks lend themselves to differentiating instruction with this activity. To get started, ask students to select one particular event from their reading and identify the causes and effects surrounding that event. For students who need more support, fill in some on the effects and/or causes on their graphic organizers. This will help students understand the type of information they should be looking for while they read.

BOOKS FOR MODELING

GRADES 2–4

The Wolves Are Back by Jean Craighead George (Dutton, 2008)

How the Ladies Stopped the Wind by Bruce McMillan (Houghton Mifflin, 2007)

Snowy White World to Save by Stephanie Lisa Tara (Brown Books, 2007)

GRADES 4–6

Tracking Trash: Flotsam, Jetsam, and the Science of Ocean Motion by Lorreen Griffin (Houghton Mifflin, 2007)

When the Wolves Returned: Restoring Nature's Balance in Yellowstone by Dorothy Hinshaw Patent (Walker & Co., 2008)

The Story of Salt by Mark Kurlansky (Putnam, 2006)

FICTION AND NONFICTION BOOKS WORK BEST WITH THIS ACTIVITY.

TECHNOLOGY

TIP ➤ A collection of organizers, including web and cause-effect patterns can be printed from Scholastic's Printables library. Find a selection for free at http://teacher.scholastic.com/tools

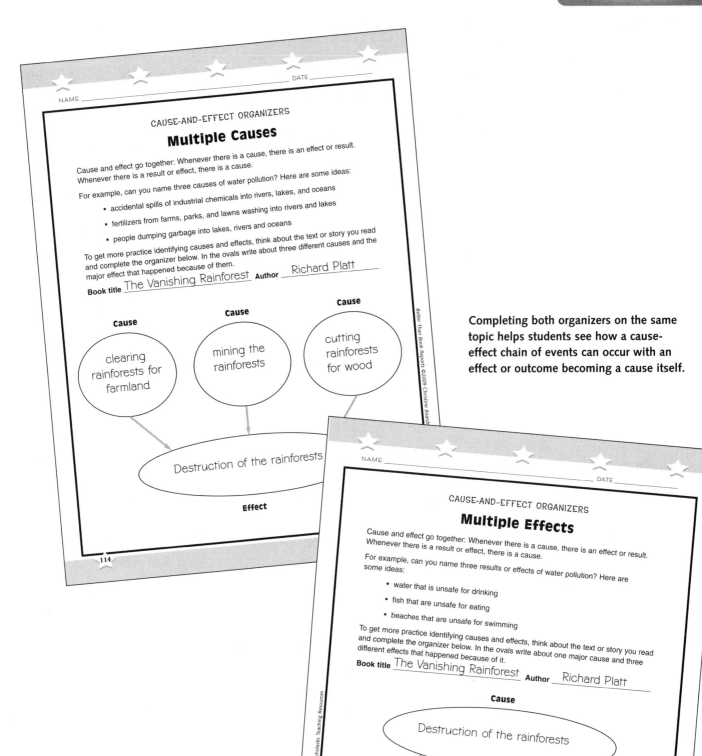

CAUSE-AND-EFFECT ORGANIZERS

Multiple Causes

Cause and effect go together: Whenever there is a cause, there is an effect or result. Whenever there is a result or effect, there is a cause.

For example, can you name three causes of water pollution? Here are some ideas:

- accidental spills of industrial chemicals into rivers, lakes, and oceans
- fertilizers from farms, parks, and lawns washing into rivers and lakes
- people dumping garbage into lakes, rivers and oceans

To get more practice identifying causes and effects, think about the text or story you read and complete the organizer below. In the ovals write about three different causes and the major effect that happened because of them.

Book title **The Vanishing Rainforest**   Author **Richard Platt**

Cause
clearing rainforests for farmland

Cause
mining the rainforests

Cause
cutting rainforests for wood

Destruction of the rainforests

Effect

114

Completing both organizers on the same topic helps students see how a cause-effect chain of events can occur with an effect or outcome becoming a cause itself.

CAUSE-AND-EFFECT ORGANIZERS

Multiple Effects

Cause and effect go together: Whenever there is a cause, there is an effect or result. Whenever there is a result or effect, there is a cause.

For example, can you name three results or effects of water pollution? Here are some ideas:

- water that is unsafe for drinking
- fish that are unsafe for eating
- beaches that are unsafe for swimming

To get more practice identifying causes and effects, think about the text or story you read and complete the organizer below. In the ovals write about one major cause and three different effects that happened because of it.

Book title **The Vanishing Rainforest**   Author **Richard Platt**

Cause

Destruction of the rainforests

floods, loss of people's homes

greenhouse effect: raising the Earth's temperature

extinction of plants and animals

Effect   **Effect**   **Effect**

113

CAUSE-AND-EFFECT ORGANIZERS

Multiple Effects

Cause and effect go together: Whenever there is a cause, there is an effect or result. Whenever there is a result or effect, there is a cause.

For example, can you name three results or effects of water pollution? Here are some ideas:

- water that is unsafe for drinking

- fish that are unsafe for eating

- beaches that are unsafe for swimming

To get more practice identifying causes and effects, think about the text or story you read and complete the organizer below. In the ovals write about one major cause and three different effects that happened because of it.

Book title _____ **Author** _____

Cause

Effect   **Effect**   **Effect**

CAUSE-AND-EFFECT ORGANIZERS

Multiple Causes

Cause and effect go together: Whenever there is a cause, there is an effect or result. Whenever there is a result or effect, there is a cause.

For example, can you name three causes of water pollution? Here are some ideas:

- accidental spills of industrial chemicals into rivers, lakes, and oceans

- fertilizers from farms, parks, and lawns washing into rivers and lakes

- people dumping garbage into lakes, rivers, and oceans

To get more practice identifying causes and effects, think about the text or story you read and complete the organizer below. In the ovals write about three different causes and the major effect that happened because of them.

Book title _____ **Author** _____

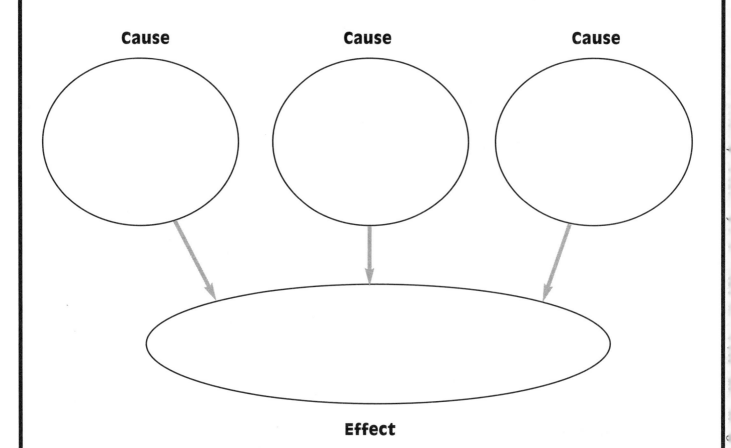

Add-On Stories

Stories that have a cumulative-repetitive text pattern support struggling readers. They learn quickly that the story is structured around a series of familiar episodes or verses with a new plot element at the end of each, as in the poem "There Was an Old Lady Who Swallowed a Fly." You can use the cumulative-repetitive text structure to help students improve fluency through repeated readings. You can also support students' writing by having students "add on" an episode to an already recognizable story.

Demonstration
& Guided Practice

Select a story that has a cumulative repetitive pattern to read aloud to the group. Then divide the class into small groups. Have the groups brainstorm additional episodes that can be added to the story and then record their episodes on paper. Ask students to take turns sharing their episodes within their small groups, a process that lends itself well to peer as well as teacher editing.

To differentiate this activity, students may wish to create their own cumulative-repetitive text structure and create original episodes in order to produce their own story books.

For more advanced readers and writers, an add-on activity might include creating an additional event in a chapter or a prologue at the end of a fiction book. In a nonfiction book, students might add a page of information on a subtopic they've researched using other nonfiction sources.

BOOKS FOR MODELING

GRADES 2–4

Who Ate All the Cookie Dough? by Karen Beaumont (Holt, 2008)

Red, Red, Red by Valeri Gorbachev (Penguin, 2007)

Badger's Fancy Meal by Keiko Kasza (Putnam, 2007)

GRADES 4–6

The Three Silly Billies by Margie Palatini (Simon & Schuster, 2005)

Nora's Ark by Natalie Kinsey-Warnock (HarperCollins, 2008)

Frog With a Big Mouth by Teresa Bateman (Albert Whitman, 2008)

FICTION BOOKS WORK BEST WITH THIS ACTIVITY.

Add-On Stories
Nora's Ark by Natalie Kinsey-Warnock

The rain kept pouring and the river kept rising. More animals and people kept coming to Grandma's big house on the hill. There were chickens and chicks, the Ferguson's horse, Major, and Mrs. Lafleur and her daughter.

Suddenly, the door burst open and in tramped Lullabell, one of the Guthrie's heifers. She was covered in mud and dripping wet! She mooed loudly, and the chickens began to squawk and the horse began to neigh.

With all the squawking and neighing and mooing, it was nearly impossible to hear Grandpa and the three Guthrie boys yell, "There's a parade of animals and people heading our way!"

Grandma and Wren looked outside. Sure enough. They saw a long line of people with baskets and all kinds of animals heading for the house.

Moooo!

An "add-on" episode for *Nora's Ark*, written by a fifth grader

TECHNOLOGY

TIP ➤ Students should word process their episodes and illustrate them. The additional pages can be put in plastic page holders and placed in the appropriate book or in a folder next to the book on your class bookshelf or library.

Research-Based ABC Books

Many alphabet books contain clever and entertaining text, full of engaging vocabulary words and appealing art or photographs. This book-sharing activity, an opportunity for students to draw on vocabulary words from their investigative reading, invites students to conduct research for an authentic purpose—to write an ABC book on a specific topic or a theme.

Demonstration
& Guided Practice

Begin by sharing with students some of the ABC books listed here or others such as Bob Raczka's *3-D ABC* (Lerner, 2007) and Steven Layne's *P Is for Princess* (Sleeping Bear Press, 2007). Point out that each book is based on a topic or a theme. Invite students to discuss the ways in which the alphabet-book format can help an author organize and provide a reader with information about a topic. Next, divide the class into small groups. Ask groups to brainstorm themes for original ABC books. Once each group has decided upon a theme, members divide up the work, noting who's responsible for which letters, and begin the research.

To differentiate this activity and involve the entire class in a collaborative project, consider creating an ABC book about your state. You can determine who's responsible for which letter by having each student draw an alphabet tile or card from a hat. Explain that students are responsible for researching and writing about a variety of topics that begin with their letter. The resulting piece should convey important information about the state. Have students write and revise their work and then embellish the ABC book with artwork.

BOOKS FOR MODELING

GRADES 2–4

G Is for Goat by Patricia Polacco (Penguin, 2007)

Stargazer's Alphabet: Night Sky Wonders From A to Z by John Farrell (Boyds Mills Press, 2007)

Superhero ABC by Bob McLeod (HarperCollins, 2008)

GRADES 4–6

Ox, House, Stick: The History of Our Alphabet by Don Robb (Charlesbridge, 2007)

R Is for Rhyme: A Poetry Alphabet by Judy Young (Sleeping Bear Press, 2005)

Yankee Doodle America: The Spirit of 1776 from A to Z by Wendell Minor (Putnam, 2006)

FICTION AND NONFICTION BOOKS WORK BEST WITH THIS ACTIVITY.

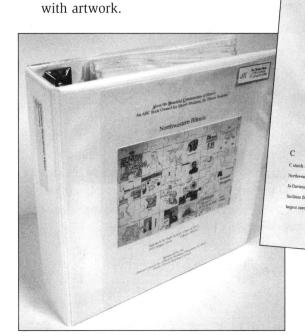

A class ABC book for northern Illinois began with a large blank puzzle. Students chose a letter to illustrate and designed their puzzle pieces based on what they had learned about their state. (The cover photograph shows the completed puzzle.) Then students glued their puzzle piece to a sheet of copy paper and wrote a caption for their letter illustration. The pages were placed in alphabetical order inside a large binder.

TECHNOLOGY

TIP ➤ The Comment feature in the program Word is used to facilitate communication between an editor and a writer. It can be a valuable tool for students to use while they work with peers to edit copy in the ABC books.

Words for Wordless Books

Being able to understand or read pictures and illustrations is an especially important literacy skill in today's technology-dependent world where graphics and icons support Internet navigation and where educators strive increasingly to address the issue of visual literacy by a variety of means, including exploring wordless picture books.

Wordless picture books captivate. With appeal to students of all ages they provide students with exceptional opportunities to imagine the thoughts, feelings, and unspoken words of each story's characters.

Demonstration & Guided Practice

One of the many ways of guiding students through this book-sharing activity is to divide the class into small groups. Give each group of students a different wordless book. Ask each group to compose a story to accompany the illustrations. Students exchange stories and books and discuss their favorite parts.

If you're more interested in having the class work on narration and dialogue, ask small groups of students to write dialogue and narration on sticky notes and place the sticky notes on the appropriate pages in the book. Student groups then exchange books and read different versions of the same story.

Another way to share wordless books with students is to divide the class into three groups. Assign each group a different section of the story: beginning, middle, and ending. One group retells or acts out the beginning of the story, another group the middle of the story, and the final group, the ending of the story. Each group is responsible for supplying appropriate narration and dialogue for their part of the story.

A way to differentiate this activity is to have students who are especially motivated or talented artistically create their own wordless books. Some students will enjoy designing their own pages, while others may prefer to use ready-made templates which are available from Bare Books at www.barebooks.com.

BOOKS FOR MODELING

GRADES 2–4

Wave by Suzy Lee (Chronicle, 2008)

Trainstop by Barbara Lehman (Houghton Mifflin, 2008)

South by Patrick McDonnell (Little, Brown, 2008)

GRADES 4–6

Flotsam by David Wiesner (Houghton Mifflin, 2006)

The Red Book by Barbara Lehman (Houghton Mifflin, 2004)

Hogwash by Arthur Geisert (Houghton Mifflin, 2008)

FICTION BOOKS WORK BEST WITH THIS ACTIVITY.

Students first filled out a sequence map to put the events of David Wiesner's *Flotsam* into words. Students then typed out the narration and dialogue that accompany each page.

(Student handwritten narration and sequence map shown)

by Sania, Ruthie, & Parker

Narration

Page 3: A boy named Cole was lying on the beach with his parents studying a hermit crab.
"Cool a hermit crab," said Cole.
"I wonder if it will pinch me".
Pg 3

Page 4: "I wonder what else I can find", Cole thought. Cole saw a crab he laid down next to the crab to examine it.
"Oh, look at this crab.
How do the arms feel?" Cole said.

Page 5: "What that sound?" Cole thought t
A wave crashed on the shore swooping Cole
"Ahhhhhhhhhhhhhh!", Cole scream

Page 6: The wave pushed Cole back
his ankles.
"That was scary!", he said in relie
"What's that?", Cole asked himself
camera with seashells on it.

Page 8: Cole picked up the camera. "
Whoooooo!" he said.

Page 9: "I wonder if I should tell my p
to his parents Samantha and Steve. C
camera. Cole and his parents went to t
never seen it before. The family went b
the case it was in. He saw the film and
"I wonder if I can get these de

Page 10: Cole ran as fast as he could. He was
could get the pictures developed. When he got to the store, a girl named Lexi was
sitting at the desk talking on the phone. "Excuse me," said Cole very loudly "Will you
print these pictures please?", he asked Lexi. Lexi opened her hand for the film.

Sequence of Important Events

A hermit crab crawls up a little boys hand → he looks and wants a picture. He keeps examining the crab then he plays image wave comics.

Suddenly, the boy hears aloud noise then a wave pushes him everything is wet Oh-no!! the boy sees on the water Camra

The boy take a closer look but there is I lim bottle i the camrea the guarad book at the cam

There is a robotic fish swimming with other fish Then there is

Octopuse has alot of friends over they ha fish over land

Little alines loading ship star fish are dancing I th

TECHNOLOGY

TIP ➤ Bring technology into play by inviting students to create PowerPoint presentations. They can do digital illustrations or try their hand at scanning their original artwork and then importing it into PowerPoint. To enhance their storytelling and add finishing touches to their narratives, students can download and add compelling background music and sound effects.

Pattern Poetry

Poetry has been referred to as "elegant shorthand" by authors and poets alike. A lot of poetry written for children is also humorous and clever, and provides opportunities for wonderful read-alouds. To help students find poems with readily recognizable patterns they can use as jumping off points for their own poetry writing, turn to the sources in Books for Modeling.

Demonstration & Guided Practice

To introduce students to using different poems for models or patterns, you might want to read Arnold Lobel's poem "I Married a Wife on Sunday" from *Whiskers & Rhymes* (HarperCollins, 1988). Prior to reading the poem, tell students to notice how the poem follows the days of the week. Point out the rhyming pattern the poet uses. Next, share "I Rode My Bike on Sunday," which appears on page 119.

Ask students to explain how "I Rode My Bike on Sunday" follows the same poetry pattern used in "I Married a Wife on Sunday." You might begin the discussion by inviting students to notice similarities and differences between the two poems. Encourage students to make observations about structure, rhyme, and rhythm.

When students can identify and compare simple patterns in poems, invite them to select a favorite poem and then write a poem of their own that follows this model. Have students peruse various poetry books, including those suggested. Provide younger students with support and guidance during their search for an appropriate poem to use as a springboard for writing.

To differentiate this activity, select a short rhyming poem to copy onto chart paper. (A pocket chart works well for this activity.) Use sticky notes to cover up one word in each pair of rhyming words. Divide the class into small groups and explain that each group will write a fresh version of the poem. They should suggest a replacement word for each word covered up and work collaboratively to create a new poem that not only makes sense, but also engages the reader. Bring students together to share results. Have a volunteer from each group share aloud his or her group's new poem.

BOOKS FOR MODELING

GRADES 2–4

Norman Rockwell: You're a Grand Old Flag lyrics by George M. Cohan ([1906], Atheneum)

Spring Things by Bob Raczka (Albert Whitman, 2007)

The Apple Pie That Papa Baked by Lauren Thompson (Simon & Schuster, 2007)

GRADES 4–6

Thanks a Million by Nikki Grimes (Amistad, 2006)

Poems in Black and White by Kate Miller (Boyds Mills, 2007)

Little Boy by Alison Mcghee (Atheneum, 2008)

FICTION BOOKS AND POETRY WORK BEST WITH THIS ACTIVITY.

TECHNOLOGY

TIP ➤ One Web site that provides interactive poetry patterns for young poets is sponsored by the Educational Technology Training Center, http://ettcweb.lr.k12.nj.us/forms/newpoem.htm.

I Rode My Bike on Sunday

by Christine Boardman Moen

I rode my bike on Sunday

Upon the sidewalk I fell.

It hurt so bad on Monday

I said that I was ill.

I rested all day Tuesday.

The bruise, it would not heal.

I rested again on Wednesday and

My sister said, "What's the big deal?"

By Thursday I felt better

And to the kitchen I hopped.

By Friday I was ready to go.

I felt I couldn't be stopped.

By Saturday I had fixed my bike.

I was walking ten feet tall.

So I rode my bike on Sunday.

And guess what? I did not fall!

Time-Telling Time Lines

Students recognize patterns and relationships within their reading by identifying important information and arranging it in sequence along a time line.

Demonstration
& Guided Practice

Explain that groups of students will be creating time lines that will graphically show the key events in a story. Divide the class into small groups of students (ideally, groups of three). Select a book from those listed here and, if possible, have all of the groups read multiple copies of the same book. If securing multiple copies proves difficult, read the book aloud to the whole class and then divide the class into groups for their small-group work on time lines.

To get started, guide students to think about important events that took place. Recording each important event on a sticky note or note card will allow students to manipulate information easily. Have students number the events in the order in which they occurred. Also, guide students as they select information to record on the time line. Probe whether the information students select is relevant to the plot and if the information has been checked for accuracy. Encourage students to use the text for reference.

Provide a partially completed time line for students who need extra support. The listed events on the time line helps guide students to complete the time line with events, dates, people, and places that occur before and after the items already listed on the time line.

When all the groups are ready to share their time lines, discuss the activity as a class. Compare and contrast the information each group has in its time line. Discuss whether any differences are significant and why.

BOOKS FOR MODELING

GRADES 2–4

A Day in the Salt Marsh by Kevin Kurtz (Sylvan Dell, 2007)

The Great Serum Race: Blazing the Iditarod Trail by Debbie S. Miller (Walker Books, 2006)

The Shepherd's Trail by Cat Urbigkit (Boyds Mills, 2008)

GRADES 4–6

The Wall: Growing Up Behind the Iron Curtain by Peter Sis (Frances Foster Books, 2007)

Tuttle's Red Barn by Richard Michelson (Penguin, 2007)

Naming Liberty by Jane Yolen (Philomel, 2008)

FICTION, NONFICTION, AND BLENDED BOOKS WORK BEST WITH THIS ACTIVITY.

Part of a time line for *Across Five Aprils* by Irene Hunt (Follet, 1964)

TECHNOLOGY

TIP ➤ Once students are done putting information in sequence, they can generate a time line using the graphic services at http://www.readwritethink.org /materials/timeline.

Going Graphic: Visual Stories

With the Caldecott winning book *The Invention of Hugo Cabret* by Brian Selznick (Scholastic, 2007), graphic novels moved into the mainstream of children's literature. The mixture of text, images, and illustrations appeals to students, especially those who spend time reading Web-based information. Helping students learn how to navigate their way through and interact with these visual stories is the purpose of this book-sharing activity.

Demonstration & Guided Practice

Divide the class into small groups and select a book to share. Take time to point out how the graphics and text support each other. Then, at different points in the story, place sticky notes over some of the text frames and ask students to supply what they think should appear in the text boxes. Ask students to explain their text suggestions and how they correspond to the images on the pages. Remove the sticky notes and compare and contrast students' suggestions.

After students have participated in this small-group demonstration and guided-practice activity, ask each student to select a graphic novel and a partner with whom to work on this book-sharing activity. To get started, students exchange books. Each student uses sticky notes to cover text boxes on three pages of his or her partner's book: one from the beginning pages, one from the middle, and one from the end. The partners then exchange books and begin the task of supplying the substitute text for each covered text box writing directly on the sticky notes. When both partners have finished reading and supplying the missing text, they can read their books together and check their suggested text boxes for logic and accuracy.

To generate dialogue ideas, partners used several sticky notes over two pages of frames from *The Time Guardian*, *Volume 1* by Daimuro Kishi and Tamao Ichinose (CMX, 2007). They then discussed the similarities and differences between the dialogue choices they and the author had made.

BOOKS FOR MODELING

GRADES 2–4

Traction Man Meets Turbo Dog by Mini Grey (Knopf, 2008)

Camp Babymouse by Jennifer L. Holm (Paw Prints, 2008)

Bone: RockJaw Master of the Eastern Border by Jeff Smith (Scholastic, 2007)

GRADES 4–6

Once Upon a Cool Motorcycle Dude by Kevin O'Malley (Walker & Co., 2005)

Frankenstein Takes the Cake by Adam Rex (Harcourt, 2008)

Magic Pickle by Scott Morse (Scholastic, 2008)

FICTION BOOKS WORK BEST WITH THIS ACTIVITY.

TECHNOLOGY

TIP ➤ Preview each graphic novel as some may not be suitable for the grade you teach. An excellent source for graphic novel review is http://www.ala.org, the URL for the American Library Association.

Press Conferences

Students are drawn into learning and participating in this interactive book-sharing activity, as they take on the guise of a person they've read about and learn from the presentations of their peers.

Demonstration & Guided Practice

With students, read one of the books listed here (or a portion of one) or select a book about an important person included in your curriculum. Tell students that a demonstration press conference has been scheduled for the following day and that you will be pretending to be the famous person featured in the book. Have each student submit two or three questions that she or he would like to ask the person. Select five to seven questions, and prepare your answers based on information in the book. The next day, distribute the questions and tell students to take turns asking them during the press conference.

To add an element of drama to the model press conference, you may dress up like the famous person or add props of some sort, although the purpose of this activity is to convey important facts and details about the person and not to present a performance. To lend an air of authenticity, try to audio- or video-record the demonstration. That way you can review it with students as they prepare for their own press conferences.

After the demonstration press conference, help students select suitable biographies. Ask students to use large note cards as bookmarks on which to record page numbers of important facts and quotations. Set a date for students to finish reading their book. On that day, hold a question-writing session. As a class, create a set of five to seven questions for each press conference. You may want to go over the questions and perhaps add one or two of your own in order to focus on certain historical events. Ask each student presenter to select at least five questions for which he or she will prepare answers and to write each question on a separate note card.

On the day of the press conference, have the student who is presenting distribute the note cards among his or her peer audience. Tell students in the audience who have note cards to take turns asking questions in a press-conference format. Record each student's press conference for viewing later and also for playing during appropriate social studies or geography units.

BOOKS FOR MODELING

GRADES 2–4

What to Do About Alice? by Barbara Kerling (Scholastic, 2008)

George Did It by Suzanne Tripp Jurman (Puffin, 2006)

Sandy's Circus: A Story About Alexander Calder by Tanya Lee Stone (Penguin, 2008)

GRADES 4–6

She Touched the World by Sally and Robert Alexander (Clarion Books, 2008)

Henry's Freedom Box by Ellen Levine (Scholastic, 2007)

A Boy Named Beckoning by Gina Capaldi (Carolrhoda Books, 2008)

NONFICTION, BLENDED, AND BIOGRAPHIES WORK BEST WITH THIS ACTIVITY.

TECHNOLOGY

TIP ➤ Show a press conference that you have recorded from television. Also, press conferences are available on the Internet at PBS and the Library of Congress sites.

A student in the persona of former Supreme Court Justice
Sandra Day O'Connor takes questions from the audience.

From Poetry to Plot

Students read a book written in verse and then write a verse-based story or narrative interpretation of the same text. This book-sharing strategy supports students' comprehension and helps them demonstrate comprehension.

Demonstration & Guided Practice

Students usually begin reading by reading rhyming and predictable texts, so reading a book written in verse is often a familiar literacy experience. However, as students grow as readers and move into chapter books and novels, they encounter verse books less often. One way to reacquaint older students to books written in verse is to read aloud Sharon Creech's book *Love That Dog* (HarperCollins, 2003) followed by its sequel, *Hate That Cat* (HarperCollins, 2008).

Once students are comfortable with verse books, have small groups of children select a book to share and write individual narratives based on their chosen book. For example, every student in one group could read *Baseball Hour* while students in another group could read *Best Book to Read*. After reading, each student writes his or her narrative based on the verse text. Older students might enjoy using the same approach with Kipling's book *If*.

An alternate approach to this activity is to use *How to Catch a Fish* with younger students and *Good Masters! Sweet Ladies!* with older students. These two books have different formats than the others on the list. Each poem in *How to Catch a Fish* is a description of how a fish is caught in a specific part of the world, whereas the poems in *Good Masters! Sweet Ladies!* are monologues by different characters in a Medieval village. You might have younger students write narratives based on selected poems from *How to Catch a Fish*. When students are done, they may read aloud the original poem and their narrative. With older students, you might have each student select one of the free verse poems in *Good Masters! Sweet Ladies!* Then he or she may write a narrative based on the text.

More mature students may want to tackle *The Brothers' War: Civil War Voices in Verse* and then read a historical fiction novel such as Gary Paulsen's *Soldier's Heart* (Random House, 2000) for a multi-layered look at the American Civil War.

BOOKS FOR MODELING

GRADES 2–4

How to Catch a Fish by John Frank (Roaring Book Press, 2007)

Baseball Hour by Carol Nevius (Marshall Cavendish, 2008)

Best Book to Read by Debbie Bertram and Susan Bloom (Random House, 2008)

GRADES 4–6

If: A Father's Advice to His Son by Rudyard Kipling, Photographs by Charles R. Smith, Jr. (Simon & Schuster, 2007)

Colonial Voices: Hear Them Speak by Kay Winters (Penguin, 2008)

Good Masters! Sweet Ladies!: Voices From a Medieval Village by Laura Amy Schlitz (Candlewick, 2007)

FICTION, NONFICTION, BLENDED BOOKS, AND POETRY WORK BEST WITH THIS ACTIVITY

TECHNOLOGY

TIP ➤ A Found Poem is a poem made up of words and phrases as well as longer passages taken from other sources such as newspapers, magazines, and books. Have students create Found Poems by taking material from their current independent-reading books. Create an audio- or video-recording of students sharing their poems aloud.

Title: _Diving Deep_   Author: _Sarah Langlois_

This story was based
on: _How To Catch a Fish by John Frank_

Wow! I'm in a snorkeling mask and fins. I aim a firing spear as I hunt along the reef below the surface of the green lagoon. I am loking for barracuda and dogtooth tuna. I hope my lungs can dive down deep in one breath. Oh no! I have to come up for air.

Two third graders take different approaches to writing a brief narrative version of a poem from _How to Catch a Fish_.

Title: _Bow and Arrow_ Author: _Caitlin Lyons_

This story was based
on: _How to Catch a Fish_

Among the reeds, dad and I hide on the Okavango River in Namibia. We wast waiting for a fish to come near. "There it is!" I yelled. Right there was a large salmon swimming around the long and skinny boat. I aimed at the fish and I shot it down. Oh No! An alligator just ait it!

Grading Rubric

Student's Name _____ Date _____

Book-Sharing Activity _____

Book Title _____ Author _____

Scoring Guide

4 **Outstanding** Student's work is creative and completed exceptionally well.

3 **Above Average** Student's work is attractive, accurate, and has few errors.

2 **Average** Student's work meets but does not exceed expected requirement.

1 **Needs Improvement** Student's work is inaccurate and/or incomplete. Many errors.

Directions

Assess criteria that apply to the book-sharing activity noted above. Refer to the scoring guide and mark the score that best describes the student's performance.

Writing Criteria

_____ Writes in complete sentences.

_____ Writes detailed descriptions, explanations, and correspondence.

_____ Supplies information to complete story frames and graphic organizers.

_____ Summarizes or paraphrases.

_____ Creates and answers questions.

_____ Other _____

Reading Criteria

_____ Comprehends and follows written directions.

_____ Comprehends different types of text structures and related genres.

_____ Identifies and explains literary elements.

_____ Comprehends and explains the use of dialogue and its purpose.

_____ Comprehends, locates, and supplies synonyms for vocabulary words.

_____ Makes predictions, rereads for understanding, and determines point-of-view.

_____ Other _____

Listening and Speaking Criteria

_____ Plans, practices, and delivers presentations for different purposes/audiences.

_____ Listens for important details and follows oral instructions.

_____ Other _____

Utilizing Visual/Media Literacy: Criteria

_____ Uses manipulatives for various purposes, such as retelling a story.

_____ Accurately completes instructions composed of visuals.

_____ Operates media devices and integrates media-created products into a presentation or demonstration.

_____ Reads a map and uses it to plot or trace a route.

_____ Utilizes photographs and illustrations for descriptive purposes.

_____ Other _____

Conducting Research/Examining Text in Detail: Criteria

_____ Searches for information within the text or a chosen book.

_____ Searches for additional information in print and non-print sources.

_____ Selects appropriate information.

_____ Other _____

Comments and/or Observations

What part of the activity did the student do well?

_____

_____

What part of the activity does the student need to improve?

_____

_____

Self-Assessment Form

Name_____ Date _____

Activity_____

Book Title _____

Author _____

Directions: Check the boxes that best describe your work. If a statement doesn't go with the activity, check the box labeled "Doesn't apply."

I did great!	I did okay.	I'll work on this.	Doesn't apply.	
❑	❑	❑	❑	I wrote in complete sentences.
❑	❑	❑	❑	I included details from my reading.
❑	❑	❑	❑	I organized information (on planning pages, checklists, or charts).
❑	❑	❑	❑	I followed written directions.
❑	❑	❑	❑	I described what happened in the story.
❑	❑	❑	❑	I explained similarities and differences.
❑	❑	❑	❑	I listened to and followed the directions my teacher said aloud.
❑	❑	❑	❑	I planned and practiced for my presentation.
❑	❑	❑	❑	I used a drawing, map, photo, or other visual.
❑	❑	❑	❑	I researched details in books, online, or another way. _____

What part of the activity did you enjoy most? Explain. If you need more room, write on the back of this page.

_____

_____

_____

About the Author

An avowed "reading warrior," Christine Boardman Moen believes in teaching students to love to read—not just how to read. Because of her efforts to nurture the love of reading, she received ICARE for Reading Award (Illinois Council for Affective Reading Education, 2003) and the Educator of the Year award (Illinois Reading Council, 2005). A classroom teacher for 25 years, Moen currently teaches 7th and 8th grade language arts in Illinois and is a grade 7–12 literacy mentor. Outside of the classroom, Moen conducts staff development across the country and serves as an adjunct associate professor of education at Rockford College. She is the author of ten professional books for teachers and one children's book, and contributes to professional periodicals, including the *Illinois Reading Council Journal*, NCTE's *Voices in the Middle*, and *Book Links*. You can visit Christine's Web site at www.chrismoen.com.